PENGUIN BOOKS

THE 80/80 MARRIAGE

Nate Klemp, PhD, is a former philosophy professor and a founding partner at Mindful. He is coauthor of *Start Here*, a *New York Times* bestselling guide to mindfulness in the real world. Nate received his BA and MA from Stanford University, and his PhD from Princeton University.

Kaley Klemp is a highly sought-after executive coach, specializing in building trusting and synergistic teams. She is also an Enneagram expert, certified Young Presidents' Organization facilitator, TEDx speaker, and coauthor of *The 15 Commitments of Conscious Leadership*. She received both her BA and MA from Stanford University.

Praise for *The 80/80 Marriage*

A *New York Times* Editors' Choice

"If you feel your relationship is unfair and you're resentful, 80/80 could save it."   —*The Times* (London)

"This book explains how to make it work."   —*The New York Times*

"Beautifully written and illustrated and brilliantly argued; any couple reading this will find themselves guided into new and challenging possibilities for their relationship, which if they take seriously and practice faithfully, will surely transform their consciousness, alter their behavior, and fulfill their dreams. We heartily encourage all couples to read it with an open mind and a willing heart."
—Harville Hendrix, PhD, and Helen LaKelly Hunt, PhD,
authors of *Getting the Love You Want*

"Times of dramatic societal change can undo close-in relationships, or strengthen them. This brilliant book offers a pathway for couples to deepen connectedness, calling forth the heart's potential for generosity, trust, acceptance, and compassion."

—Tara Brach, author of *Radical Acceptance*
and *Radical Compassion*

"Now more than ever, modern couples struggle to find love and connection in the midst of the complexities of modern life. *The 80/80 Marriage* offers a powerful solution. It gives couples practical tools for shifting out of keeping score and striving for fairness to a mindset of radical generosity."

—John Gray, author of *Men Are from Mars, Women Are from Venus*

"One of the central struggles in modern relationships is the illusive sense of fairness. *The 80/80 Marriage* gives couples a new, more effective model for navigating this terrain, and a powerful way to begin feeling more connected and in love."

—Lori Gottlieb, author of *Maybe You Should Talk to Someone*

"Nate and Kaley Klemp, through their own marriage and interviews with scores of couples, give us a fresh perspective on handling the age-old issues of intimate relationships: communication, chores, money, sexuality, and more."

—Gay Hendricks, PhD, coauthor of *The Big Leap* and *Conscious Loving* (coauthored with Dr. Kathlyn Hendricks)

"What's fair is not always equal and what's equal is not always fair. Nate and Kaley offer approachable exercises to shift from a 50/50 mindset to a relationship mindset, creating respect and true appreciation for every twenty-first-century couple." —Eve Rodsky, author of *Fair Play*

"*The 80/80 Marriage* takes us beyond the inevitable power struggles and the scarcity mentality of so many modern relationships. It is a brilliant way forward to deeper love and lasting happiness."

—Doug Abrams, coauthor of *Eight Dates* and *The Book of Joy*

"This book will be hugely helpful to everyone except divorce lawyers. It's filled with profound insights about reframing your relationship, along with specific tips on everything from date nights to chore dividing to screen avoidance. Thank you for writing it."

—A. J. Jacobs, author of *The Year of Living Biblically*

"The core insight of this book is of vital importance: good marriages depend on virtues beyond fairness. Equality is not enough: only generosity will do. And a narrow focus on equality can get in the way. Nate and Kaley have written a book with important lessons not only for marriages, but partnerships and communities of all kinds."

—Stephen Macedo, Laurance S. Rockefeller Professor of Politics at Princeton University and author of *Just Married*

"Nate and Kaley Klemp's *The 80/80 Marriage* offers a new model of marriage for a new generation of couples. Instead of arguing over fairness, they call for a shift to a mindset of radical generosity. Instead of asking, 'What's best for me?' they call for a shift to a spirit of shared success. It's the perfect step-by-step guidebook for making relationships work in the modern age—not just at home, but throughout all of our lives."

—Chip Conley, *New York Times* bestselling author, strategic adviser to Airbnb, and founder of the Modern Elder Academy

"Kaley and Nate take a headlong dive, fearlessly and with humor, into the assumptions underlying the 'modern marriage.' Drawing on recent research and a wide range of personal interviews, they help us see why so many of our views of how marriage ought to work are flawed. The prescription they arrive at leaves lots of room for our different personalities and inclinations, but its core premise—putting 'us' before 'me' and 'you'—is compelling and inspiring."

—Barry Boyce, founding editor of *Mindful*
magazine and Mindful.org

"*The 80/80 Marriage* offers an original framework for thinking about marriage success based on a fundamental spirit of generosity. It's worked for us!"

—Lauren Smart, retired finance executive, and Dr. Geoff Smart,
chairman of ghSMART and *New York Times* bestselling
author of *Who* and *Power Score*

"Entrepreneurs and busy professionals face the constant challenge of trying to achieve success at work while also staying connected to their partners at home. *The 80/80 Marriage* offers a powerful solution. It's a practical guide for creating a new mindset and structure in marriage built to handle the pressures of real life."

—Brad Feld, cofounder of the Foundry Group, and coauthor
(with his wife, Amy Batchelor) of *The Startup Life*

"*[The 80/80 Marriage]* will take your marriage to the next level!"

—Tommy Spaulding, *New York Times* bestselling
author of *The Heart-Led Leader*

"In a world focused on the self, it's refreshing to see a solid plan for couples to unselfishly work together."   —*Booklist*

THE

80/80

MARRIAGE

A New Model for a Happier,
Stronger Relationship

NATE KLEMP, PhD, AND KALEY KLEMP

life

PENGUIN BOOKS

An imprint of Penguin Random House LLC

penguinrandomhouse.com

First published in the United States of America by Viking,
an imprint of Penguin Random House LLC, 2021
Published in Penguin Books 2022

A Penguin Life Book

ISBN 9781984880796 (paperback)

THE LIBRARY OF CONGRESS HAS CATALOGED THE HARDCOVER EDITION AS FOLLOWS:
Names: Klemp, Nathaniel J., 1979– author. | Klemp, Kaley, author.
Title: The 80/80 marriage : a new model for a happier, stronger
relationship / Nate Klemp, PhD, and Kaley Klemp.
Other titles: The eighty marriage
Description: New York : Penguin Life, 2021. | Includes bibliographical references.
Identifiers: LCCN 2020024766 (print) | LCCN 2020024767 (ebook) |
ISBN 9781984880772 (hardcover) | ISBN 9781984880789 (ebook)
Subjects: LCSH: Marriage. | Married people—Psychology. |
Intimacy (Psychology) | Communication in marriage.
Classification: LCC HQ734 .K624 2021 (print) | LCC HQ734 (ebook) |
DDC 306.81—dc23
LC record available at https://lccn.loc.gov/2020024766
LC ebook record available at https://lccn.loc.gov/2020024767

Printed in the United States of America
2nd Printing

Set in Sabon MT Std
Designed by Cassandra Garruzzo

Some names and identifying characteristics have been changed
to protect the privacy of the individuals involved.

To Margi, Joe, Judy, and Jim,
our models of love

CONTENTS

PART 4:
Living the 80/80 Marriage

INTRODUCTION

It all started with a pair of smelly running shoes.

When we first moved in together at the age of twenty-four, Nate used to leave his running shoes piled up by the front door. Each day, he'd casually walk into the condo and kick them off, sending them flying across the floor to land randomly in a clump near the doormat.

One day, after a week of living together, Nate went to grab his shoes. But they were gone. He searched the closets, the garage, the porch, and the garbage can. No luck.

"Have you seen my shoes?" he asked Kaley.

"I told you, it drives me crazy when I walk into the house and trip over them. I feel like your maid and that's not fair. So now you're going to have to find them," she said.

Annoyed by this game of hide-and-seek, Nate continued his search. Twenty minutes later, after rummaging through the entire condo, he found them tucked away on the top shelf of the kitchen cabinets, those high-up shelves above the refrigerator ordinarily reserved for useless appliances.

Now Nate was pissed. He charged into Kaley's office. "Are you serious? I just spent twenty minutes trying to find my shoes."

Kaley swung around in her office chair. "I told you, it drives me nuts when you don't put your shoes away. And it's not my job to put away your crap."

One week in and the fight for fairness—the fight over who's doing more and who's doing less, who cares more and who cares less—had begun.

From Shoe Drama to In-law Drama

As the years passed, Nate learned to put away his shoes. But soon, new and more complex conflicts emerged.

After getting married at the age of twenty-six, we would travel home during every holiday season to spend time with both sets of parents in Colorado. To make things fair, we brokered a time-sharing deal that seemed like a stroke of genius: Nate's parents got Christmas Eve and Christmas Day. Kaley's parents got the three to four days after Christmas. Since Nate's family got "the two holidays," Kaley's family got the next two days plus a you-missed-the-real-holiday bonus day or two for not getting Christmas. The deal seemed perfectly fair. Quid pro quo.

There was only one problem with this bargain: it left open the question of the exact, down-to-the-minute time we left Nate's family's house on Christmas night. From an outsider's perspective, it seems so trivial. *Who cares whether you leave at six p.m. or seven p.m.?* But one Christmas morning, the question turned nuclear.

"I'd really like to be in the car by six so that we make it to my family's house before everybody goes to sleep," Kaley said.

"Babe, Christmas dinner isn't over until at least seven, and I don't want to rush out of there while everyone's sitting at the dinner table," Nate replied.

That's when fairness crept into the conversation.

"We're spending Christmas Eve and all of Christmas Day with your family. I'm just asking to leave a few minutes early so we can at least say hi to my family on Christmas," Kaley protested.

"Yeah, but we're spending two extra days at your parents' house," Nate replied. And on and on it went.

Each year, we dreaded that fateful hour of transition. Each year, we fought the same battle, which boiled down to this: "What you're asking for isn't fair."

The Fight That Almost Ended It All

Six years into our marriage, things got even more complicated. We had a baby girl, and suddenly we weren't just bickering over the mundane tasks of domestic life and extended family logistics. Now the entire structure of our lives—from our finances to our work ethic to our careers to what we did during our increasingly rare "free time"—was up for grabs.

We soon discovered that we had no clue how to answer some of the most basic questions in married life: Who pays the credit card bill? Who cooks dinner? Who books airplane tickets when we travel? Who schedules our daughter's dentist appointments? Who takes care of her when she's sick? And who picks her up from daycare?

That last question almost ended our marriage.

One warm September night while we were sitting in the garden-lined patio of a local Mediterranean restaurant, Kaley asked Nate, "Can you do pickups at three thirty a few times a week this fall?"

But that's not what Nate heard. He interpreted the question as something more like "Since you're a writer who doesn't have a real job, can you end your workday early to get our daughter?"

Nate reacted by launching into a rant about not being respected. Kaley fired back with all the reasons she felt unappreciated. Then there were several digs about Kaley traveling too much and a few more about Nate not caring enough.

That's when we lost it. It reached a point where the whole thing felt so unfair, so insane, that Nate dropped all remaining traces of his ordinarily Zen persona and blurted, "I don't care what you think. I'm not changing the way I live my life."

With that, Kaley left the table to cry in the bathroom.

One day later, we could barely talk to each other. One week later, the rage and resentment still lingered. It would take the better part of a year to clear away the emotional wreckage created by this fight—over what? A daycare pickup time?

Looking back, it's now clear. This fight had nothing to do with picking up our daughter. It was about something deeper: fairness.

This fairness fight almost ended our marriage.

But it's also the fight that led us to change it.

The Battle for Fairness

How about you? While the details might not be the same, have you and your partner fallen into this trap? How much time and energy gets sucked away by conflicts over what is or isn't fair, over who's doing more and who's doing less, who cares more and who cares less? How often do you fight about things like a daycare pickup time, whose friends you're spending Saturday night with, a purchase that seems extravagant, or a forgotten run to the store to get more eggs?

In the aftermath of our daycare pickup fight, we wondered if we were the only ones struggling to find a way out of this battle or whether this pattern was something more universal, a challenge faced by all modern couples.

We had to ask because when we looked on Facebook and Instagram, it seemed like we were all alone, lost in the woods of marital dysfunction. We didn't see anyone else talking about their struggles. All we saw were glorious photos of couples on vacation, lounging alongside an infinity pool, cocktails in hand, having the time of their lives. We read dazzling anniversary posts in which one partner would publicly declare their unshakable love for the other, garnering hundreds of likes and "You guys are amazing!" comments. Posts like these made us wonder, "Are we the only ones having trouble figuring this thing out? Is everyone else off backpacking in Montana, having tons of sex, and living happily ever after?"

To answer these questions, we decided to turn from social media to real conversations. We conducted formal interviews with more than one hundred people from all walks of life.[1] We talked to couples who seemed to have the perfect marriage, couples struggling to save their marriage, couples who had recently divorced, and couples who chose not to marry. We talked to artists, academics, teachers, scientists, stay-at-home parents, CEOs and corporate executives, progressives, conservatives, Christians, atheists, heterosexual couples, same-sex couples, and one set of nomads on a seven-year honeymoon, living out of a van.

In the end, it didn't matter what they did in their career, how much money they had, or whom they voted for. The more we looked beneath all those glossy posts on social media, the more we witnessed, both in ourselves and in others, an insight that changed everything: Everyone seems a little bit lost when it comes to making marriage work. Everyone seems to be searching for a better model—any model, really—for being equals and managing the chaos of modern life, all while staying in love.

We also discovered that most modern couples grapple with a similar list of challenges. Almost everyone we spoke with reported living in a constant state of busyness, a harried feeling of never having enough time. One woman told us, "I go through life just wishing someone would give me an hour." Another told us, "I'm used to getting an A-plus in life, but I'm so spread thin right now that everyone in my life—my husband, my kids, my employees—gets a C or a C-minus from me."

They also reported feeling overwhelmed, confused, and exhausted by the demands of balancing marriage with parenting, caring for aging parents, and advancing in their career. One man told us, "With all that's going on, I get to Monday at the end of the weekend, and I'm never refreshed, not at all." One woman told us, "It's impossible. I have no solutions. Balancing all of this is the hardest part of my life."

And just about every couple reported that these pressures have taken a toll on their relationship. One man told us, "We're so enslaved to our calendar that it's hard to figure out how to find time to be with each other." One woman even confessed, "Honestly, sometimes my husband is talking and I'm not listening at all. I'm so distracted and so exhausted from the day that I don't hear a single word he is saying."

This is the condition of modern marriage. We're trying to be the perfect partner, all while keeping up with the dizzying pace of life, working in an "always on" environment, and waking up each day to posts about the friend who just finished a marathon in record time (while also raising twelve thousand dollars for cancer research).

No wonder it's so hard.

To make things worse, the go-to strategy promoted by our culture for finding balance is the very same tool that almost ripped our marriage apart: the idea that if we just make everything fair, then we'll finally live in a conflict-free state of marital bliss.

And that's the real problem. This seemingly noble marital aspiration to make things fair causes us to fight about whether a thirty-minute shopping trip to Home Depot counts as weekend "free time." It's what causes us to argue over who's going to stay home with our kid, who just projectile-vomit-stained the living room carpet. And it's what causes us to fight about the fact that one of us has been working hard to save money while the other just walked in with a three-hundred-dollar robot vacuum cleaner for the kitchen.

The more time becomes scarce, the more tension builds. The more stress we add to the system, the more toxic this battle becomes, and the further we fall from being in sync, connected, and in love.

Is There Love After Fairness?

On some level, every modern couple has to navigate this treacherous path. We're all trying to figure out how to treat each other as equals, balance our individual ambitions, and stay in love. This has certainly been our challenge.

We're both in our early forties. We've been married for fifteen years but have been together, on and off, for the past twenty-four. Since the day we met in chemistry class during our senior year of high school, we were told that we owed it to ourselves and the world to "realize our potential" and "do great things" (as individuals, of course). This led Kaley to build a career as a highly sought-after executive coach. It led Nate to become a professor, then a writer and entrepreneur. Oh, and one last thing that's probably worth mentioning: in each of these years, Kaley out earned Nate, often by a factor of five.

We're not like our parents, who had time for hobbies and midweek adult racquetball leagues—we're constantly pressed for time. And while our grandparents might have been content with a dependable and steady partner, we want our spouse to be, well, everything—a best friend, an amazing lover, a rock-star parent, a kick-ass professional, a dedicated family and logistics partner, as well as a daily source of support, kindness, fun, and inspiration.

Like most modern couples, we want to have it all. We want individual success with all the benefits of sharing a life together. We want large stretches of time for being fully present with our child. We want to feel connected and in love. We want to relax, whatever that means. In short, like many of the couples we interviewed, we've continually bumped up against the wall of reality, the infuriating fact that *it's impossible to have it all*.

So what are we to do? How can we change the game of marriage and relationships so that we can have more of what we really want—deep love, equality, and connection—and less of the endless battle for fairness?

The 80/80 Marriage is our answer. It's the product of fifteen years spent using our own lives as a laboratory to test out tools for optimizing marriage in the modern age. It's the product of extensive interviews with couples from all walks of life. It's the product of decades spent using our work with corporate executives and high performers to better understand the relationship dynamics of this new generation of couples. And it's the product of years of conversations with the world's leading experts on marriage as well as in-depth research on the science of marriage.

The Three Models of Marriage

How did we get here? And where are we to go? In this book, we're going to take you on a journey through three models of marriage.[2] Each model represents a different way of forming a life together.

In chapter one, we'll explore how we got here, via the 80/20 model. Think 1950s Pleasantville, a time when rigid and unjust gender norms defined marriage. The man's job is to work, achieve, and provide. The woman's job is to raise the kids, manage the social calendar, and make sure her husband comes home to a clean house and a wonderful meal each evening. In this arrangement, women contribute 80 percent, if not more, of the time, energy, and emotional work of marriage. Men get away with 20 percent. While the problems with this model are now painfully obvious, we'll examine the subtle structural virtue of this arrangement that has fallen away over the past seventy years.

In chapter two, we'll explore where we are now, the 50/50 model. Thanks to a growing consensus around gender equality, both partners now have the cultural stamp of approval to become a hard-charging executive, a path-breaking scientist, or a rock star. The result is a model of marriage and relationships based on fairness, one in which each partner is expected to contribute equally to a marriage. The virtues of this model are obvious. Our current aspiration to equality in marriage is an undeniable improvement over the blatant sexism and injustice of the past. And yet there are deep problems that arise when we try to achieve equality in marriage by keeping score and making everything fair; we'll examine some of these in what's to come.

In the rest of the book, we'll delve into where we want to go next: the 80/80 model. An 80/80 marriage involves a shift in the spirit of contribution. It's a way of being equals while also staying in love and improving our ability to manage the unique challenges of the modern age. With an 80/80 marriage, each partner strives to contribute 80 percent. We know that this makes no logical sense. There's no such thing as a 160 percent whole. But the irrationality of this goal is sort of the point. The only way to break free from the current cultural obsession with fairness in marriage is to work toward something radical. We think 80/80 is the answer. The rest of the book will explain why.

This move toward an 80/80 marriage involves two big shifts. The first is a shift from a mindset of fairness to one of radical generosity, which shapes what we do, what we see, and what we say. The second is a shift away from the restrictive roles of the 80/20 model and the confusion of the 50/50 model to a new structure, one organized around shared success, designed to help us navigate roles, priorities, boundaries, power, and sex more skillfully.

The 80/80 marriage is radical and may not work for everyone. And yet we think it's worth trying because it changed our lives forever. Our marriage still requires constant work. We still have good and bad days. We still disagree and argue about things. And yet these tools have helped us stay connected and in love, even during the rockiest patches of life.

We think they will do the same for you.

Who This Book Is For

Even though we talk about three models of marriage, you don't have to be married to benefit from this book. You could be engaged, in a committed relationship, or in the early stages of dating. All couples, married or not, confront some variation of these challenges and can benefit from making the shift to an 80/80 model.

You also don't need to be in a heterosexual relationship. While some of what we talk about relates to roles dictated by socially constructed gender expectations, the 80/80 model applies to all relationships between two equal partners.

The strength of your current relationship—or lack thereof—also doesn't matter. If you're doing well in your relationship, this book will help you optimize the mindset, structure, and habits of your shared life.

If you're in a period of conflict and crisis, this book offers a path out of the struggle.

And finally, it doesn't matter whether you both work or one of you stays at home. There are all sorts of work arrangements in modern marriages, from the single-breadwinner model to the dual-earner, two-career model to the primary-secondary model, in which one partner works full time and the other part time.[3] No matter the arrangement, all of these couples are striving for a better way to be equals while staying in love.

Ultimately, there's only one qualification for reading this book: an interest in improving your intimate relationship.

What if you want to change but your partner couldn't care less? This is a real problem, one that many people experience. The problem, of course, is that it takes two to shift the mindset and underlying structures of marriage. We've included a chapter called "Resistance—The Reluctant Partner" (chapter fourteen) to help you determine whether the 80/80 model can work for you and explore how it can benefit you even if your partner isn't yet fully on board. We have also included tips throughout the book to help you open up a deeper conversation with your partner about the value of updating to this new, more fulfilling way of being in a relationship together.

How to Read This Book

This book is structured around four key parts. The first discusses the three models of marriage we've shared. The second explores the mindset shift that sits at the core of an 80/80 marriage, a shift from fairness to radical generosity. The third part outlines a new structure for married life based on shared success. The final part offers practical steps you can take to apply the concepts from this book in your everyday life.

You can, of course, skip around. However, if you choose to do so, we recommend that you at least begin with our discussion of radical generosity in chapter four, as it sets the stage for creating the structure and new habits that go along with an 80/80 marriage.

At the end of some chapters, you'll find a practice. These practices are your opportunities to reflect, try out new ways of thinking, explore new structures, and challenge your ordinary assumptions about marriage. While you can do these alone, we recommend doing them with your partner so that you can explore the ideas together. How you engage with these practices is up to you. For some readers, it makes sense to pause at the end of the chapters with a practice and try it out, even if only briefly. For other readers, it might work best to read the entire book and then return to the practices that offer the most value. Find an approach that works for you.

Finally, as you will soon see, we have built the framework of this book out of both our own experiences and the experiences of others through extensive interviews. In some cases, we use the real first name of the interviewee. When the subject is a public figure, we use their last name as well. And, in some cases, we have changed the name and identifiable details at the request of the subject to protect their anonymity.

Why Should You Read This Book?

If you're reading this book, chances are you're like the one hundred or so people we interviewed, busy and pressed for time. You have to-dos to check off, emails to write, errands to run, and more. That can make the idea of taking the time to read this book seem almost irrational. After all, just think how much other stuff you could get done.

But here's why we think it's worth it. Spending the rest of your days with another human being is a wild ride through the good and the bad of life that can leave you worse off, lost in resentment and irritation, and relieved when it's finally over. Or it can open you up to new worlds of experience, joy, fun, creativity, ecstatic pleasure, and meaning.

And if there's one thing we have learned from the journey of researching, writing, and living the practices in this book, it is that investing wisely in your relationship pays out huge returns. You get less of the
energy drain and stress that come from living in a state of constant tension and conflict. You get more of what you really want: love, connection, and intimacy.

And that, paradoxically, might not just make you happier in your
relationship. It might also help you get more done.

PART 1

Exploring the Three Models of Marriage

CHAPTER 1

80/20—Where We Were

Long before Dr. Ruth and Dr. Phil, during a time when nobody talked publicly about sex and the inner workings of marriage, there was Dr. Edward Podolsky, a pioneer in the field of self-help and marriage advice.

One of his most popular volumes was his 1945 book, *Sex Today in Wedded Life*. The book reads more like an anatomy text than a racy modern sex manual. It offers "confidential" advice on everything from debunking "the harmfulness of masturbation" to the frequency of sex in marriage to the embarrassment some men feel when their scrotum retracts after taking a dip in a cold pool.

And yet, in the two closing chapters, he offers what might just be the best distillation of the inner ethos of what we call the 80/20 model: ten commandments for wives and husbands.

When it comes to his list for husbands, his advice seems dated but not altogether culturally backward:

- Remember your wife wants to be treated as your sweetheart, always.
- Don't be stingy with money; be a generous provider.

- Compliment her new dress, "hair-do," cooking, etc.
- Always greet her with a kiss, especially when other people are around.[1]

Taken as a whole, these tips might not exactly hit the mark when it comes to modern marriage advice. But they're also not totally crazy.

That is, until you read some of his commandments for wives:

- Be a good listener. Let him tell you his troubles; yours will seem trivial in comparison.
- Remember your most important job is to build up and maintain his ego (which gets bruised plenty in business). Morale is a woman's business.
- Never hold up your husband to ridicule in the presence of others. If you must criticize, do so privately and without anger.
- Don't try to boss him around. Let him think he wears the pants.[2]

What's most amazing about these marriage commandments is that from one phrase to the next, they move from sound relationship advice to wildly sexist claims that even today's marriage traditionalists see as going too far.[3]

"Don't ridicule" your spouse in the presence of others—that's actually good advice. "Be a good listener"—again, great tip. And yet in the very next line, the shadows of the 80/20 model emerge. Because right after "Be a good listener" comes "Let him tell you his troubles; yours will seem trivial in comparison." Lines like these tell you just about everything about the status of men and women in this model.

Dr. Podolsky's marital utopia is a world where men and women live together like master and servant, CEO and secretary, provider and maid. The ideal woman is a domestic service worker. Her job is to cater to the whims of her husband. If he's hungry, cook him a fabulous meal. If he leaves his jacket on the floor, hang it up in the closet. If he's stressed after a long day at the office, be his private chef, escort, and at-home therapist.

Virtue and Vice in the 80/20 Model

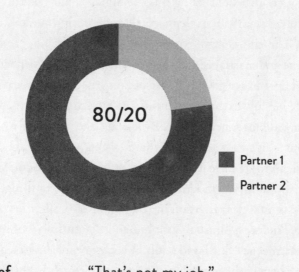

Belief	"That's not my job."
Mindset	Deference and Control
Structure	Rigid Gender Roles

The 80/20 model is designed around asymmetrical power and inequality. One partner, historically the woman, takes on 80 percent of the burden while the other, historically the man, puts in 20 percent or less. The woman defers. The man has control. Everyone knows their place.

You might ask: What is this ratio measuring? What does doing 80 or 20 percent in marriage represent? This ratio is a measure of the spirit of contribution. It's a spirit that includes the typical domestic stuff—childcare and work around the house. But it also includes more intangible forms of contribution, such as the effort, energy, and emotional output required to keep the marriage moving smoothly in the right direction. These ratios, in other words, are a measure not only of who's doing the dishes but also of who's managing conflicts, looking ahead to big decisions, and thinking of ways to strengthen the marriage.

There's a core belief fueling this dynamic: "That's not my job." This is what makes the 1950s-style manifestation of this model so much like servitude. The wife isn't an equal—her job is maintaining the well-being of the home and marriage, and she's on the hook for 80 percent. She can't pursue her dreams outside the house because that's her husband's job. And because of her low earning potential and lack of financial resources, it's almost impossible for her to leave. By leaving, she would have no job at all.

Of course, it's easy to see all that's wrong with this model. What's more difficult to spot are its virtues. In spite of all the problems with this arrangement, the 80/20 model actually does a couple of things quite well. First, it rests on a clear division of roles and responsibilities. Cooking—wife's job. Finances—husband's job. Being delightful—wife's job. Manning the barbecue—husband's job. That's not an endorsement of the outright sexism in this model. But it's an important insight to remember as we begin to look toward the 80/80 model.

There's one other virtue of the 80/20 model: unified direction, even if it's a direction set solely by the man. Couples have clear incentives to work together toward common goals. If you're a man, you want your wife to excel at raising the kids and setting a fantastic table for guests. If you're a woman, you want your husband to get that exciting new promotion at work. All this is to say that in spite of its many problems, the 80/20 model is set up to incentivize something positive: a spirit of shared success.

Life After the 80/20 Model, or "Why Am I Still Doing Everything?"

From the vantage point of modern times, the 80/20 model may seem both like the beginning of marriage history and like some sort of cultural throwback we have moved far beyond.

In truth, both of these ideas are false.

Until just a few hundred years ago, around the eighteenth century in the West, marriage was pretty different from the 80/20 model. Of course, these earlier models of marriage shared the extreme inequality found in the 80/20 model, often in an even more amplified form. But they didn't involve some of the big marital innovations that culminated in the 1950s. Couples in the ancient past mostly lacked the ability to choose a mate. And romantic love—the core aspiration of marriage in the twentieth century—had almost nothing to do with the decision to marry. Instead, marriage throughout most of history was about maximizing your chances of survival, securing economic advantages, or, for those lucky one-percenters of the distant past, building political alliances.[4] So from the perspective of history, the 80/20 model of coupling, in which marriage is chosen and often based on some idea of romantic love, is actually distinctly modern.

The idea that we've moved beyond the inequality of the 80/20 model is also false. As Sheryl Sandberg points out in *Lean In*, there's a vast gap between the *promise* of equality and *true* equality.[5] Take, for example, the business world, where women are told that they are equals but are consistently paid less than their male counterparts and often overlooked for executive-level positions.[6]

This gap between the promise of equality and true equality also defines the world of modern marriage. Almost everyone in the industrialized world believes in the *promise* of gender equality. A recent Pew survey, for instance, found that 97 percent of Americans support the idea.[7] But that's just what we *say* about gender equality in marriage, not what we *do*. When we look at the reality of modern marriage, we see that the unequal and unjust 80/20 model is alive and well today, living on beneath the surface in even the most progressive households.

How does this milder, gentler form of 80/20-style inequality manifest today? In our interviews, we found that at times, it's clear and easily identifiable. But mostly, it shows up in invisible ways, harder to see but no less corrosive on our aspiration to marital equality.

The Easy-to-See Hangover of the 80/20 Model

To see this form of inequality in action, consider Abby and Dave. They met during their junior year of college. At the time, Dave was one of those hard-partying frat guys, the type who play beer pong at an elite level but lack many of the most basic life skills to survive as an adult. At twenty years old, for instance, Dave had never even washed his own dirty clothes. Instead, each weekend, he would make the twenty-minute pilgrimage to his parents' house, where his mom would wash and fold his laundry for him.

Abby lived on the other extreme of the life-skills polarity. Unlike Dave, she had long since mastered the art of operating a washer and dryer. She managed her own finances, booked all her own travel home to see her parents, and had developed elaborate systems for keeping track of important bills, deadlines, and other to-dos.

So when Abby and Dave fell in love, they also fell into a pattern in which Abby did, well, just about everything. Abby got Dave a credit card because he didn't seem to have the will or interest to do it himself. She bought plane tickets for him because, again, he couldn't seem to do it himself. Within a few years, this pattern shifted from an every-once-in-a-while nuisance to the central theme of their relationship.

Twenty years later, Abby and Dave still live like they did in college. Even though Dave now works in consulting and Abby has the bigger job with the bigger salary as CEO of an international organization, she still does everything. As Abby describes it, "I'm the CEO. I'm the primary breadwinner. But I'm also the one who's making sure my child is taken care of and managing everything around the house. While he's lying on the couch and I'm doing all the work at eight months pregnant, he doesn't even offer to help. But nor do I ask. Because if I demand it, I would have to be willing to leave the marriage. And that is an unfortunate place to always be in."

It's easy to see what makes this setup so problematic. At home, Abby's

doing the very same thing wives in the 1950s did: all the work of managing a house and raising kids. But unlike the apron-clad 1950s housewife,
she's also working sixty- to seventy-hour weeks as the CEO of a large
organization. She's working two jobs, while her husband spends his post-
work hours working through seasons of *Breaking Bad*.

We could hear the frustration and strain in Abby's voice. At one
point, she confessed, "My husband is a lost cause. I've now set up my
life with so many workarounds that I don't even need him anymore."

Not all couples live with such extreme inequality. And yet the most
recent data shows that when it comes to the amount of time spent on
household work, most heterosexual couples are indeed far from achieving equality. The Pew Research Center, for instance, reports that the
average dad now spends around eight hours on childcare and ten hours
on chores each week. The average mother, on the other hand, spends
eighteen hours on childcare and eighteen hours on chores each week.[8]
While the gap between how much women and men contribute has been
closing steadily over time, women still do more.

The Invisible Hangover of the 80/20 Model

The inequality in Abby and Dave's marriage is easy to see. But this isn't
always the case. Many of the most powerful forms of inequality fly
under the radar. They're difficult to see but no less destructive to the
promise of equality in marriage.

This more hidden form of inequality isn't about who spends more
time on housework and childcare. It's about who spends more mental
and emotional energy on it. It's a difference that matters because most
tasks in domestic life aren't hard to do. For instance, it's not hard to
pay your cell phone bill. It's not difficult to renew your driver's license.
It doesn't take a PhD to figure out how to pick your kid up at the bus
stop.

And yet hidden behind the thousand or so trivial tasks of domestic life is something that actually is hard: the mental and emotional burden of making sure these mundane tasks get done. It turns out that it's much more difficult to remind your spouse to pay the cell phone bill every month—and deal with the emotional experience of irritation that arises in both of you—than it is to actually pay it. It's more difficult to make sure that you've met the gluten-free, keto, and vegan eating needs of guests at an upcoming dinner party than it is to make the salad and tofu. Managing, remembering, and navigating the emotional strain of these everyday tasks requires mental and emotional work. Getting them done, by contrast, is a mostly automatic form of physical labor.

This may sound obvious. But it's a subtle difference that eluded even the brightest minds in psychology and sociology until just recently. As more and more women entered the workforce, researchers started to see that there was more to domestic inequality than time spent on the physical labor of household tasks. They realized that even when men and women spent the same number of hours on household work, something was still amiss—women still seemed to be the "designated worriers."[9]

University of California, Berkeley, sociologist Arlie Hochschild realized that we needed a name for this invisible form of work and dubbed it *emotional labor*.[10] We asked her about the difference between emotional labor and other kinds of work. She told us, "Emotional labor has to do with who's handling the tensions, who's mindful of them, and who takes it as their work to make everything run smoothly."

The kind of work Hochschild describes is mostly invisible and often difficult to track. It's not the *physical* work of actually putting away dishes or changing diapers. It's the *emotional* work of worrying, planning, navigating family tensions, and mentally scanning the future for playdates that need to be scheduled to support your kids, dinners that need to be scheduled to stay in connection with old friends, or parents who need to be called on their anniversary.

Because emotional labor exists outside time and space, during our interviews we often noticed it in the strangest of places. Consider James, a self-described progressive man. He's emotionally sensitive, a staunch supporter of women's rights, and the first to support female candidates for office. And yet in the process of scheduling a time for him and his wife, Stephanie, to talk with us, he responded in an email with the following one-liner:

As always, I'll let Stephanie schedule for us. ;)

We could give you pages of interview data, but this one line says it all. "I'll let Stephanie schedule for us" is his way of saying, "She carries the burden of scheduling." "As always" is his way of signaling that having her run point on life logistics isn't some one-off event. It's the unconscious atmosphere of their relationship, the air that they breathe in their marriage. And when it comes to the winking emoticon at the end, well, we're not sure what to make of that.

To be clear, James probably isn't saying "I'll let Stephanie schedule for us" to be a jerk. He's saying it because the whole idea of emotional labor is so slippery, so surreptitious, that he, like many men, may not even be aware that it's happening.

The Same-Sex Advantage

When talking with both same-sex male and same-sex female couples, we encountered a common theme: when you're married to someone who shares your gender, you often don't have to deal with the cultural baggage of the 80/20 model.

Consider Danielle and Paige. They've been together for several years and were just months away from becoming parents of twins when we spoke with them. When we asked about the cultural baggage of traditional roles, Danielle explained, "We have a certain freedom from traditional gender roles. There just aren't the same expectations put on us by society to have kids or get married. And that leaves us with more freedom to do things the way we want to and find a more natural fit around roles." Paige shared the same view. "The baggage from society," she told us, "isn't there."

Male same-sex couples echoed this same theme. As one man told us, "Because we're both men, we don't have this built-in expectation set based on gender that we're fighting against. We both approach marriage with fresh eyes."

The Conservative Christian Rejection of 80/20

We learned one other surprising insight about the 80/20 model from talking to couples. Many deeply conservative Christian couples also reject the basic assumptions of this model. Time and time again, these so-called traditional couples referred to the "dated" values of the 1950s as a thing of the past. As Greg Smalley, vice president of marriage at the conservative Christian organization Focus on the Family, told us, "There may be pockets of Christians who still believe in this kind of gender inequality. But I don't know of anyone in my community who would disagree with the basic premise of equality in marriage. From a purely biblical standpoint, God created us the same. We're just as valuable, just as important."

A conservative Christian woman told us her story of actually lamenting the loss of her old 80/20 life. When she and her husband moved to a new city, they both applied for jobs and, in the end, she got the better job with the higher salary. That's when her husband proposed an idea that shocked her: "What if I stay at home?" As she told us, "I remember being really surprised at that idea, and there was some real resentment for a while that I had my stay-at-home job taken out from under me. It took me a while to see that this new arrangement was actually a really good thing for our family."

Conservative Christian activists promoting gender equality in marriage and conservative families switching the husband to a stay-at-home role—this isn't the mainstream narrative about the nature of marriage on the far right of the political spectrum. And yet it's what often surfaced in these conversations.

All this is to say that when it comes to the hangover of the 80/20 model in modern life, it's complicated. That's why we've taken this model as our starting point. It's a messy reminder that we haven't fully left it behind. Statistically speaking, in heterosexual marriages, men still do less and women still do more. These cultural facts matter when it comes to restructuring marriage—they are basic facts we will return to as we explore the new, more promising model of 80/80.

CHAPTER 2

50/50—Where We Are Now

Tom and Sarah are the quintessential 50/50 couple. They both have big dreams and ambitions. They both believe in equality in marriage. And as a result, they're both committed to doing marriage differently than their parents did.

Fairness, you might say, has become their most sacred principle. It shows up in big things: how they spend, save, and invest their money; how they discipline and parent their kids. It even shows up at the most microscopic level, like the seemingly trivial question of who's keeping an eye on the kids and who's able to roam free, engaging in undistracted adult conversation, at get-togethers with their friends.

Tom and Sarah's parents had an elegant but unfair solution to this question. Mom's job at such events was to be on permanent daycare duty. Dad's job wasn't really a job at all. He would do just about anything he wanted while all the moms sat together near the kids, bantering about parenting tips and neighborhood gossip.

Tom and Sarah aren't like their parents. They want their marriage to be less like a kingdom and more like a democracy: equal, fair, and just. So to solve this problem, they did what any clever 50/50 couple might do. They created a system to achieve cocktail party conversational fairness—a system that was straightforward, perfectly egalitarian, and totally absurd.

At these events, they set a repeating timer for ten minutes to "tag-in and tag-out." For the first ten minutes, Tom might be on kid duty, while Sarah had time to dive into deep conversation with her best friend about a problem she faced at work. Then, with the chime of the cell phone timer, their roles instantly reversed: Tom got his turn to roam free, while Sarah went back to kid duty. Tag in to watch the kids, then tag out to talk to your friends—all great, so long as each person gets equal time.

This exquisite system worked, until it didn't. As you might expect, conflict soon arose over breaches of the ten-minute rule. When one person got more social time, the other felt irritated and resentful.

These violations of the ten-minute rule, however, weren't the real problem. The real problem was with the principle underlying the system itself. Fairness, after all, might just be the perfect principle for running a government or divvying up money when a relative dies. But when it comes to the messy business of creating a life together with kids, careers, pets, and parents, Tom and Sarah's story shows just how quickly 50/50 fairness starts to break down.

The Declaration of Marital Fairness

Tom and Sarah didn't invent this battle for fairness. If anything, Alix Kates Shulman did.

The year was 1972. Alix and her husband lived in New York City with their two small children. With the birth of their two kids, Alix's husband's life stayed the same. He had the same job and the same freedom to leave their apartment for long stretches each day. Alix's life, meanwhile, turned into a kind of domestic sweatshop—a six a.m. to nine p.m. daily grind filled with trips to the Laundromat, two-year-old meltdowns, and visits to the pediatrician.[1]

Inspired by the burgeoning women's liberation movement, Alix decided to make things fair. What resulted was "A Marriage Agreement"—

a multipage marital contract describing in excruciating detail a full inventory of who does what, when, and how. "As parents," she declared, "we must share all responsibility for taking care of our children and home." Jobs, she insisted, "should be shared equally, 50/50." What happens when one partner ends up doing more than the other? Alix's answer was payback: "He/she must be compensated by equal extra work by the other."

The agreement establishes precise times, days of the week, and payback rules for mornings, transportation, helping the children, nighttime routine, arranging babysitters, sick care during the workweek, weekend kid responsibility, cooking, shopping, cleaning, and laundry. When it comes to helping the kids with homework, for instance, "wife" does Monday, Wednesday, and Saturday; "husband" does Tuesday, Thursday, and Sunday. Friday goes to the person who has a lingering fairness debt to pay down.[2]

The marriage agreement reads like a 50/50 manifesto. And at the time of its first publication, in 1972, it struck a cultural nerve, sparking outrage and intrigue in the broader culture. *Life*, *Redbook*, and *Glamour* magazines all published versions of the essay.[3] Alix instantly became a feminist hero to some and a target of ridicule by others.

We tracked down Alix Kates Shulman, who is now eighty-eight years old and still living in New York City. She admitted that this agreement might seem extreme. But, she told us, "at the time, a woman couldn't even go into an upscale restaurant without being accompanied by a man because she would be presumed to be a prostitute." It was an era when, in her words, "the idea that a man should do any kind of housework or childcare was considered emasculating, degrading, and laughable." These conditions led early feminists like Shulman to fight for a new vision of marriage based on equality and 50/50 fairness.

It was a vision made possible by several broader cultural changes in the decades following the 1950s. The rise of the birth control pill in the 1960s, for instance, meant women had greater sexual freedom and the ability to control when and how they started a family. They could now more easily choose to postpone marriage until after college or getting a job.[4] This new freedom allowed many women to break out of their 80/20 role as wife, mom, and homemaker and claim a more equal status.

Shifts in the economy also meant that women now faced lower barriers to entry in the workforce. In 1950, women made up 30 percent of the workforce. By 1970, that number rose to just under 40 percent. By the year 2018, women made up nearly half (47 percent) of the US labor force.[5] What's more, in 31 percent of US households in 2018, women earned as much as or more than their husbands.[6] With more women entering the workforce and a growing number of them out earning their husbands, the single-breadwinner model of 80/20 started to break down. Many working women now had the confidence and economic freedom to resist the idea of doing 80 percent, which meant their husbands could no longer get away with doing only 20.

All of these changes upended the traditional 80/20 model, setting the stage for a new model of marriage, one that looked less like reruns of *Leave It to Beaver* and more like Alix Kates Shulman's marriage agreement, a model based on 50/50.

Virtue and Vice in the 50/50 Model

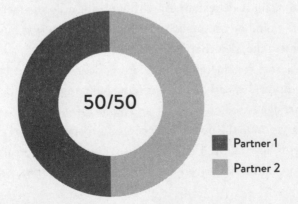

50/50

Partner 1
Partner 2

Belief	"When you win, I lose."
Mindset	Fairness
Structure	Role Confusion

The 50/50 model represents a giant leap toward greater gender equality, a shift from the outright sexism of the 80/20 model to a more just arrangement. It's grounded in fairness and achieves equality with a simple bargain: "I'll do my 50 if you do your 50." That's the real virtue of this setup. This move toward fairness in marriage helped begin to pry apart the shackles of the 80/20 model at a time when women were first entering the workforce.

But that's only part of the story. As you may have found in your own relationship, the 50/50 mindset of fairness also has its vices. Instead of encouraging us to work together toward a common goal like the 80/20 model, it often pits us against each other. Now that we both have the freedom to start a business, get promoted at work, or earn an advanced degree by going back to school at night, we're often pulled in opposite and conflicting directions by our separate goals, plans, and ambitions. When I get that big new promotion that might require us to move, I win, you lose. When you go off on a weekend trip with your friends, you win, I lose. It's a zero-sum mentality that shapes the central 50/50 belief: "When you win, I lose."

This kind of motto is fine in business or sports, where the goal is to compete against your opponents and win. But in marriage it's a disaster. It turns us against each other, making us competitive rather than supportive, jealous rather than grateful, resentful rather than loving. As one woman in an ambitious two-career couple told us, "I live with the fact that my husband will always be resentful of my success in business. That's tough to work through."

Excess individualism and envy aren't the only problems. The 50/50 model also represents a shift from the clarity of the 80/20 model, in which everyone knows their role in the system, to a state of chaos and role confusion. We're now equally responsible for everything: making money, raising kids, and all the thousands of random tasks of domestic life. And this leads many couples to bicker constantly about who did what, who did more, who cares more, or who's trying harder, because it's never clear what is or is not fair. And sure, you could write out an elaborate contract like "A Marriage Agreement," but as the story of Tom and Sarah at the beginning of this chapter shows, that often just leads to more scorekeeping, more resentment, and more marital unrest.

The Many Faces of Fairness

How does the fight over fairness show up in your relationship? It's a question worth asking because fairness is often invisible. It's clouded over by powerful emotions such as irritation and resentment. This can be a real problem, because when you don't even know you're fighting over fairness, these conflicts become far more difficult to resolve.

When you see it happening, by contrast, you gain a new freedom. You now have a choice: you can keep waging this unwinnable war, or you can shift your mindset from this 50/50 fixation on fairness to one that's more productive (more on that in the next chapter).

So the first step to unwinding this habit is to see it happening in real time. To do that, it can be helpful to explore some of the classic ways this modern fight shows up. Each marriage, after all, has its own battleground over fairness. For some, it's household chores. For others, money. For still others, it's about sex, status, or respect. But in the end, these fights for fairness generally manifest in six ways.

- **The Domestic Scorekeeping Fight:** The classic 50/50 dispute, this is a fight over who does more and who does less when it comes to all the tasks of domestic life: vacuuming up dog hair on the couch, replacing the half-and-half that just went bad, or waiting around for the cable guy to show up during a three-hour service window on a workday. It's a fight that sounds something like this: "I just canceled an important meeting to be here for the cable guy. The least you could do is take over the ballet class carpool." Translation: I'm pissed because I did more than my 50 percent, and now you owe me.

- **The Friends and Extended Family Feud:** This is the fight to find the perfect 50/50 balance between time spent with your family and friends and time spent with your partner's family and friends. You'll know you're in this one when you hear lines like "You said you're tired of going to dinner at my parents' house and now you're asking me to spend a long weekend with yours. Are you serious?" Translation: We need to spend the exact same amount of time with our extended families to hit 50/50 perfection—not a minute more, not a minute less.

- **The Money Fight:** Subtler but potentially the most explosive, this is the fight that happens when your partner returns with an armful of shopping bags from Nordstrom Rack, while you haven't shopped for new clothes in a year. It's the feeling you have when you buy your dad a thirty-dollar sweatshirt from Old Navy for his birthday and your partner buys his dad a five-hundred-dollar tournament-grade Ping-Pong table. It's the nuclear argument that occurs when you tell your partner, who's working sixty-hour weeks, that you want to take a "work sabbatical" for a few months to figure out your next move. You'll know you're experiencing the money fight when you hear: "I can't believe you spent that much," "Why are you such a cheapskate?" or "Why am I grinding every day while you're sitting around doing nothing?" Translation: I'm mad because I'm doing more than my 50 percent by saving while you're spending. Or if you're the other partner: I'm mad because you're too cheap.

- **The "You Think You're More Important Than Me" Fight:** This one's all about power. It happens when one person's professional accomplishments force the other to take on more domestic work, accommodate in various ways, or lose their voice. This argument erupts when your partner's new job offer threatens to uproot your family and forces you to change jobs, or when your partner, who out earns you, decides they should be the one to pick where you go on your next vacation. Why? Because they make more than you. It's the rage that rears its head when your partner books a three-day business trip and nonchalantly says, "While I'm gone, can you run across town to pick up my dry cleaning?" Translation: Because my career or time is more important than yours, I get a pass on the rules of 50/50. It's your job to work your life around mine.

- **The Free-Time Tiff:** This fight starts happening the day you leave the hospital and walk through your front door with your first child. In this moment, "free time" changes from being a relatively abundant resource to something more like domestic gold—scarce, hard to find, and insanely valuable. It's the fight that starts with a line like "You already had your time. You went to Target without the kids. Now it's my turn to go for a run." Statements like this elicit a predictable response, something like "Yes, you're right. I went to Target. But that's not 'my time.' That's me buying a bunch of stuff for the family." Translation: Free time during nights, weekends, or family vacations needs to be distributed 50/50. Oh, and what you call my "free time" isn't actually free time at all.

- **The Battle over Blame for Past Harms:** This fight lies deep in the subconscious realm of married life, so deep that it's often impossible to name. When levels of resentment rise and tempers flare, the conversation often turns into a prolonged fairness battle over past harms. "You're the one who said that horrible thing," says one partner. To which the other replies, "Well, you're the one who did that other horrible thing." This fight is like a courtroom drama. Each party puts forth evidence of how the other person is the real problem, all to prove that they were right and their partner was wrong, that they acted honorably and their partner messed up, or that they were the victim and their partner was the clear villain. It sounds like "You were the one who walked out on me that night," or the predictable reply, "Yeah, I did walk out because you were the one who screamed at me in front of the kids." Translation: You did something worse than what I did. You were more out of line than I was. That wasn't fair, so now you owe me.

Take a moment to consider which of these fairness fights (and there could be several) show up in your relationship. It may also be that you experience other fairness fights that aren't even on the list. The goal in doing this is to build awareness—to see these fights more clearly so you can begin to notice them happening in real time and shift the pattern.

The Two Fallacies of Fairness

Catching yourself in the act of fighting for fairness is an important first step. The next step is to consider an even bigger question: Why do these battles over fairness never seem to go away? It took us decades of looping through these same fairness fights before beginning to see the answer. After years of arguing about who should be texting the babysitter, who should shovel the snow off the driveway, and who should be planning extended family events, we started to see that fairness isn't real. It's like a mirage in the desert—it looks like it's there, and if you just go far enough, you'll find it. But it's an illusion.

This mirage of fairness is so seductive that there are entire books about it. You can learn tips and tricks on how to write your own marriage agreement. But this doesn't solve the problem, because the more we try to make things fair, the more miserable we become. Why? It comes down to two problems.

Problem 1: Comparison

Have you ever heard someone make absurd comparisons across different and totally unrelated fields? It sounds something like this: "Who's the better musician: Mozart, John Coltrane, or Katy Perry?" Not only are these questions annoying, they make no sense. They're attempts to compare people's contributions across radically different areas of expertise and even different periods of history.

This might sound like a strange habit, one that you rarely slip into. But if you look closely, you may find that this pattern sits at the core of many of your conflicts. In relationships, it turns out, we're constantly comparing our efforts to our partner's and trying to keep score. But the problem is that we're not playing just one game, we're playing around seventy different games at a time. On any given day, the work we do includes household tasks, buying groceries, yard work, picking up the dry cleaning, work at the office, family finances, taxes, vacation planning, childcare, planning social events, taking a day off to be with a sick child, coordinating with extended family, hosting holidays, volunteering at school, and on and on.

Trying to keep an accurate marital scorecard is a lot like trying to identify the one best team in the NBA, NFL, NHL, MLB, pro bowling, the World Cricket League, and about fifty other sports. It's impossible. You can't score touchdowns in hockey. You can't keep score when you're not even playing the same game.

Here's how this problem might show up in your day-to-day relationship: Imagine you've just spent the past two hours of a Saturday afternoon reconciling bank statements and preparing end-of-year finance reports for taxes. Meanwhile, your partner just strolled through the door after spending a couple of hours with friends, either getting a massage or watching football at a sports bar.

You might see this as unfair. Why should you spend your Saturday afternoon lost in Quicken reports while your partner is off having a great time? And if you feel this strongly enough, you might even call them out: "I just spent the last two hours doing our finances while you were out having fun with your friends."

But this statement, like most 50/50 marital scorekeeping, makes no sense. You're comparing your work on finances to your partner's work on finances. Even worse, you're limiting the comparison to the past couple of hours. You're saying things are unfair, but you're looking at only one marital game. You're ignoring your partner's contributions in all other areas, at all other times—their calls to upgrade the speed of the wi-fi, a late-night trip out of bed to get your kid a glass of water, or the hour they spent mowing the lawn earlier. You're also not taking into account the fact that contributions in marriage are inherently lumpy over time. Sometimes you do more, sometimes your partner will do more. That's just the way it goes. The reality of modern marriages is that we are each doing so much, across so many different areas, that it becomes extremely difficult to say what is or isn't fair.

Problem 2: The Contribution Blind Spot

Suppose there was some way to magically solve the comparison problem— an elaborate algorithm for keeping score across the hundreds of conflicting domains of household work. It would still be impossible to determine what is or isn't fair.

The problem? It turns out we're really bad at calculating how much our partner does and even how much we do around the house. When it comes to our partner's contributions, our estimations are distorted by the limited information we have available to us. It's a phenomenon that cognitive psychologists call *availability bias.*

In marriage, you witness firsthand each email, text, crumb picked up off the floor, or school drop-off that *you* do. When it comes to what your partner does, things get fuzzy. You might occasionally see them coming home with an armload of groceries or spending an unknown amount of time planning after-school activities or a vacation. But most of the data is unavailable to you. The result is that you're intimately aware of what *you* do, but more or less clueless about what your partner does.

To make matters worse, psychologists started noticing in the late 1990s that we're not just blind to our partner's contributions, we're also deluded about our own. When it comes to what we do around the house, we consistently overestimate our contributions.[7] We say we spent ten hours watching the kids, when it was really six. We say we spent three hours shopping when it was really more like ninety minutes. And here's the real kicker. In all these studies, while both men and women consistently overestimate their own contributions, men do it more—a lot more.[8]

We asked UNC Charlotte professor Jill Yavorsky, one of the world's leading experts on the subject, "Why are we so bad at making these estimates of how much we contribute around the house?" She told us we're bad estimators for two reasons: "first, parenting can be so exhausting that it just feels like we're working more than we actually are, and second, our work around the house isn't continuous. We're actually better estimators of the time we spend working in the office because it's more continuous. Childcare, on the other hand, is often off and on and involves so many moving parts that it's difficult to pinpoint the actual time spent on household work." Yavorsky's point is that because tasks like childcare and housework are so tiring and happen in such a choppy, on-and-off way, we turn out to be really bad at estimating how much of it we actually do.

Let's take a step back and just consider what all this means. The comparison problem makes it so we're never comparing apples to apples. It's more like we're comparing apples to gluten-free avocado toast. And even if we could make sense of it all with accurate comparisons of our work versus our partner's, it wouldn't matter because we're basing our claims to fairness on faulty assumptions and unreliable data. We're blind to our partner's contributions and prone to significantly overestimate our own (particularly if we're male).

And as if that weren't bad enough, there's one additional problem with this 50/50 attempt to make everything fair: not all childcare and housework is a grueling chore that nobody wants to do. Some of this "burden" we're trying so hard to distribute fairly is actually fulfilling. Some of it is work we *want* to do.

Harvard professor Jane Mansbridge, one of the leading scholars of feminist political movements, led us to this surprising insight. She told us about the moment she and her husband returned from the hospital with their baby boy some forty years ago. After dinner, when the time came to clear the dishes and change the baby's diaper, she asked her husband which he would prefer to do. He said he didn't care. Then she thought to herself, "To heck with feminism; I *want* to change that diaper and be with my baby."

"I've been an active feminist all my adult life," she explained to us, "but I was not going to let that stand in the way of the few extra minutes I could be with my son."

This is the paradox of the 50/50 marriage. It represents a huge leap forward from the unjust and outdated gender norms of the 80/20 marriage, and yet there's so much more to love than keeping score and making everything fair. That's why it's worth exploring a new model of marriage, one that not only extends the 50/50 promise of equality but also adds a new mindset and structure built to amplify love, intimacy, and connection in the midst of modern life.

We think the 80/80 model of marriage is the answer. The rest of the book will help you understand why.

CHAPTER 3

80/80—Where We Want to Go Next

Like most couples, Priti and Ankit had to chart a new path once they got married, from the inherited models of their parents to a new, more updated model. Unlike most couples, however, they couldn't just tweak the models of their childhood. They had to build something entirely new.

Both Priti's and Ankit's parents met in India before immigrating to America. While Priti and Ankit met on a dating app, their parents hadn't dated at all. Their marriages had been arranged.

In the beginning, Priti and Ankit struggled to make sense of this clash between Indian tradition and American individualism, between the culture that shaped them at home and the culture that shaped them in college, on social media, and at work. "We would get into major arguments and disagreements about fairness every few days," Ankit recalls. "I would think to myself, *Why am I the one who took the trash out the last three times? Why am I the one who mopped the floors four times? Why am I the one doing all the dishes and chopping all these vegetables?*"

Priti experienced similar challenges. One year, they agreed to divide Mother's Day and Father's Day. Priti's family got Mother's Day;

Ankit's family got Father's Day. It sounded like a perfectly fair, 50/50 deal, and yet, as Priti told us, "We were working out the timing of the weekends and Ankit said, 'For my folks, let's go on Friday. For the weekend with your parents, can we please go on Saturday?' And I was like 'Why would we go on Friday for your family and on Saturday for mine?' And what's so messed up about it is that I didn't even necessarily want to go to my parents' house on Friday. I just wanted it to be fair."

Arguments like these led Priti and Ankit to realize that the more they debated the down-to-the-minute balance of time spent with extended family or the number of hours spent chopping vegetables, the more they experienced anger and resentment. As Priti put it, "We became accountants when things weren't fair."

With no clear model to fall back on, Priti and Ankit found their own way out of this cycle. They started by changing their motivation. Instead of fairness, they started experimenting with doing even the most mundane household tasks from a spirit of generosity and love. "Now, in situations where I'm the one mopping the floor or taking out the trash," says Ankit, "I try to do it out of love, realizing I'm helping us both."

They also started to see themselves more like a team. During a recent conversation about whether they would leave Chicago for one of their careers, for instance, they quickly shifted from fairness to this new, bigger perspective, and it opened up a world of possibilities. "We realized," Priti said, "that if a move is good for the family, we would do it. And that's how we ended up resolving the discussion. We could both see that even if the chips didn't land on our individual side, it's because the move is in service of something bigger—our union."

What Thriving Couples Know

We learned many things from interviewing hundreds of people about the wild ride of managing kids and careers, the pressure of never having enough time, and the challenges and joys of sharing a life together. The most valuable insight from all these conversations? *Thriving couples have a different way of doing marriage.*

The happiest couples we spoke with had left behind the asymmetrical power dynamics and outdated gender roles of the 80/20 model. They all talked about the importance of things like equality, sharing responsibilities, and being a team. But achieving 50/50 equality was just the beginning.

These happy couples had also moved beyond many of the traps of the 50/50 model. In one woman's words, "This idea of fairness in marriage is like a football game where everybody is fighting to be the quarterback. But if everybody is the quarterback, then who is he throwing to? Where is the offensive line? And how do you ever win the game?" The couples who thrived, in other words, could see that fairness turned out to be the obstacle in marriage, not the goal.

Instead, they talked about moving beyond fairness toward a radically different mindset and structure of marriage. They described a shift from 50/50 to an 80/80 model of building a life together.

The 80/80 Marriage:
A Radical New Relationship Ratio

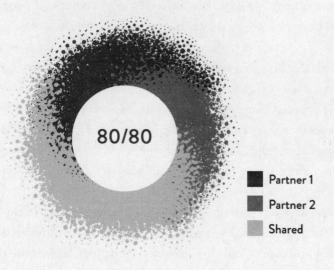

	Partner 1
	Partner 2
	Shared

Belief	"When you win, I win."
Mindset	Radical Generosity
Structure	Shared Success

If 50/50 is the ratio of fairness, 80/80 is the ratio of radical generosity and shared success. Each partner strives to contribute 80 percent, for a combined whole of 160 percent. We realize that the math doesn't work. But think of it this way. From the mindset of 50/50 fairness, 100 percent is the outer limit of love, connection, and creative potential. As you can see in the diagram above, the 80/80 model pushes us beyond these limits. The combined 160 percent represents a new world of marriage. It blows up the assumptions and the math of the 50/50 model to give us access to deeper love, connection, and intimacy.

With the 80/80 marriage, we shift from the 50/50 belief "When you win, I lose" to a new belief: "When you win, I win." We leave behind the idea that we're two ambitious individuals charting separate paths, falling back on fairness when conflicts arise or when we don't get our way. We shift instead to a true partnership, in which we move together, rather than apart, through the challenges of work, parenting, and romantic love.

As you will soon see, this new model works on two dimensions. The first is internal. It's what we call *mindset*. Mindset is how we think, feel, and interpret this daunting task of building a life with another person for decades to come. Going from 50/50 to 80/80 involves a mindset shift from fairness to radical generosity. As one man told us, "We don't think in terms of fairness. Instead, we're both bending over backward to be contributors and help each other out. My wife just told me that the fifth-grade moms are setting up a bake sale to raise money for the school and my first instinct was 'How can I help?'" This spirit of bending over backward for your partner is the essence of radical generosity.

The second dimension of the 80/80 model is external. It's what we call *structure*. Structure includes all the operations, logistics, responsibilities, rituals, and practices that allow us to stay connected in the midst of the chaotic flow of life. The 80/80 structure organizes roles, priorities, boundaries, power, and even sex around the idea of shared success. It's an 80 percent effort to prioritize your goals together over your own. As one woman described it, "The mistake I see happening over and over is thinking about *you* instead of *us*." Another woman noted that the key to her marriage was understanding that "if you have a success, it's two people that have the success, not one." In short, all of life in the 80/80 model is structured around a shift from me to us, from individual to shared success.

Mindset and structure fit together like the software and hardware on your computer. When they're in sync, we're creative, efficient, and connected. When glitches emerge in either area, your work together in marriage is a lot like trying to design your family Christmas card on one of those 1980s pale gray, first-generation Macintosh computers: slow, inefficient, and painful.

When we shift to an 80/80 mindset and structure, by contrast, we stop burning so much energy on pointless arguments and screaming matches. We can now direct all that creative power toward common goals that make us both better: financial stability, raising happy kids, impacting the world in a positive way, going on adventures, and having outrageously good sex.

Why Not 100/100?

If you want to get radical, why not push the edge of generosity all the way? Why not design a 100/100 system of marriage in which both partners aspire to put in 100 percent?

The answer is that 80 percent is meant to push the edge of your generosity. It's meant to break up all the old habits that keep you anchored in the 80/20 or 50/50 model. But pushing this edge is a lot like stretching your hamstring—it's good to push to the edge of the stretch, but if you push it too far, you might hurt yourself.

In this case, the risk isn't that you will end up hobbling around with a pulled muscle. It's that you will go so far in the direction of generosity and selflessness that you end up experiencing the dangerous opposite: losing your own identity, preferences, or purpose.

There is, in other words, the possibility of both underdoing radical generosity and overdoing it, which is why we're setting the bar at 80 percent instead of 100. One man we interviewed used the metaphor of a bus to explain this risk of going too far—of pushing toward 100 percent and losing yourself. In his words, "I got on the bus of marriage and kids without ever really thinking about it. That's just what I was supposed to do. I never asked, 'What do I want?' and that has caused all sorts of problems in my life." The dilemma expressed by this man was one of overdoing altruism. He gave up so much that he ended up losing himself.

So while the 80/80 model is meant to push the edge of your generosity, it stops at 80 percent as a reminder that you can be both radically generous and individually fulfilled.

Why the 80/80 Model?

Before embarking on the mindset and structure of the 80/80 marriage, we want to give you an even deeper answer to the question we posed at the end of the introduction. It's the question that goes something like this: "I'm already overwhelmed by my life. I have hundreds of other to-dos and priorities begging for my attention. So why should I spend time and energy on this new model of marriage? What return can I expect from this investment into improving my relationship?"

To answer this question, consider three of the main benefits you can expect to experience from this shift to an 80/80 marriage.

The 80/80 Model Redirects Energy from Conflict to Creativity

Think about the last knockdown, drag-out argument you had with your partner. Think about how much time and energy it required, and the toll this cascade of stress hormones took on your work, parenting, and health, not to mention your partner's. Living in a state of perpetual conflict with your partner is akin to living in an emotional war zone. It's a relentless source of stress, anxiety, anger, and unease.

Of course, much of the conflict we experience in married life is subtler, less like a plate-breaking rage fest and more like a low-grade hum of passive-aggressive resentment and stress. But even these more minor tensions eat away at our life energy. They're like a shoe that doesn't quite fit right. After a day of walking, your heel has a small blister. After a month, it's a bloody mess.

When we shift the mindset and structures that create this constant unease, we experience an exponential increase in energy. We're now working *with* each other instead of against each other. As a result, we're each more creative, productive, and alive. We not only achieve more as individuals, but we begin to achieve collective levels of success we never could have imagined. And we now have more energy left over to invest in friendships, children, and other activities that impact the world.

The 80/80 Model Opens Space for Greater Intimacy

The 80/80 model is based on the idea that the boring logistics of managing a house and the sublime experience of amazing sex are closely connected. It may not seem like packing lunches, organizing playdates, and cleaning leaves out of the gutter influence your experience in the bedroom. But as we will see, how we manage the mundane affairs of life has everything to do with how well we connect in our most intimate moments.

When you're lost in fights over fairness, feeling resentment and anger toward your partner, the whole thing just isn't very sexy. And that shows up across all of life, not just in line at Costco but also while lying together in bed on a Sunday morning.

When you're able to shift the underlying mindset and structure of your relationship, you may begin to experience the kind of sexual charge you felt during the early days of your relationship, only this time it's deeper, more mature, and longer lasting.

The 80/80 Model Helps Us Change the World by Changing Our Marriage

With so many devastating challenges facing the world—hunger, climate change, global pandemics, and political unrest—it may sound selfish to spend your time and energy improving your relationship. But consider the cost of a struggling marriage. It starts with the mental and emotional strain both partners experience. The collateral damage grows from there, extending like ripples on the surface of a still pond to the couple's children, parents, siblings, friends, and entire community of coworkers and acquaintances. It changes the world, but not in the way they want.

By working toward a healthier marriage, we move from impacting the world through our suffering to impacting the world through a shared sense of love, joy, and purpose. We model something radical—a marriage built on generosity and shared success—for our children and perhaps even generations beyond. When we invest in this work, we're not just improving our marriage. We're creating positive change in the world.

What the 80/80 Model Is and Isn't

The 80/80 model *isn't* couples therapy.

We are huge fans of couples therapy. It helped our marriage during several periods. Even now, when we hit a rough patch, one of the first things we do is call our therapist. The 80/80 model, however, isn't the same as couples therapy. It's not about resolving a specific dispute. Instead, it's a model for shifting the underlying mindset and structure of the entire marital system to create room for fundamental change. So you might still need counseling even if you've mastered the 80/80 model. You might still need the 80/80 model even if you have an amazing couples therapist. The two work together, on different levels.

The 80/80 model *isn't* a guidebook for unwinding past traumas.

Our relationships are inevitably shaped by past scars and traumas, both from childhood and from previous relationships. The 80/80 model can help you shift the underlying mindset and structure of your relationship. But it's no substitute for working with an experienced therapist who can help unwind these deeper psychological knots.

The 80/80 model *is* a guide to navigating the challenges of modern relationships.

Traditional marriage books focus on essential relationship skills such as listening, giving, appreciation, emotional awareness, and navigating conflict, tools that work independent of time and place. The 80/80 model, by contrast, focuses on the specific context of modern life, a context in which many couples find themselves stuck in a fight for fairness. The goal of the 80/80 model is to build a new mindset and structure, designed to meet the needs of our modern age. It refers to some of these traditional marriage skills but also explores nontraditional tools designed to enhance married life in this nontraditional time.

The 80/80 model *is* a journey into the lived experience of greater love and connection.

Each idea of the 80/80 model attaches to a corresponding practice, an experiential tool designed to help you integrate the concepts of this new model into everyday life. As you move through these practices, you will discover new skills, insights, and rituals. You will go beyond just reading and thinking about generosity, connection, love, and intimacy. You will experience the power of these tools firsthand.

These benefits of the 80/80 model sound great in theory. But where do you even begin?

The answer is mindset.

PART 2

Cultivating
a New Mindset

CHAPTER 4

Radical Generosity—The 80/80 Mindset

Here are two quotes from two different people in two very different marriages. As you read them, ask yourself: Which relationship seems to be working out better? Which relationship would you rather be in?

RELATIONSHIP 1

From the moment we had kids onward, we were always out of step. We live with a constant mismatch of expectations. Even when he could easily help, he won't volunteer. He rarely says, "I can pick up the kids today," or "I will take care of this." That is, until it becomes an ugly battle. Everything rests on a tacit understanding that I do more. I manage our finances. I do our financial planning. I do playdates. I've taken it all on. He will never even initiate a conversation about who is going to drive the kids to their activities, which says to me that he doesn't see it as his responsibility. And when it comes to my career, he's one of those guys who always say, "I will never get in the way of your career." But his actions tell me that I can't take up a more challenging role at work because the kids will suffer.

RELATIONSHIP 2

The day we moved in together, we were sharing a bathroom for the first night. We were standing there by each of our sinks, and he turns to me and says, "What is our decision on whether or not we want to leave the toothpaste on the counter or put it in the drawer?" And I thought, "Oh my God! I love this man!" It's the little things. He's super helpful. He unloads the dishwasher and does so much for the kids. If he goes to the gas station to wash his car, he will pick up a little card and write me a couple of sentences thanking me for being an amazing mom and wife. The card then shows up in my purse later that day and I think to myself, "I am so lucky." These small gestures go a really long way. Both of us are willing to go 99 percent of the way for the other. And we do that by going out of our way to do little things here and there: unexpected compliments, surprise notes, and other small acts.

Reading these two quotes is like entering into two different worlds. The first world lies somewhere between 80/20 and 50/50. You can sense the 80/20 residue of old-school and unjust gender norms. At the same time, you can also sense the friction, resentment, and tension that come from the 50/50 expectation that things *should* be—but clearly aren't—fair. It's a world where you feel constantly let down, frustrated, and upset. From the moment you wake up, it's as if you're just waiting for your spouse to say something totally messed up or fail to follow through on an important task, yet again.

The second quote gives us a glimpse into the world of 80/80. Life in this second world feels smoother, brighter, and more vibrant. Marriage sounds, well, amazing. It's a world where you wake up wondering what you can do to support, delight, engage, or even turn on your partner. You're not worried about doing more than your fair share in this world, nor is your partner. Your partner becomes your mirror, reflecting your own kindness and generosity at every turn.

The shift between these two worlds is like the shift from black-and-white to color TV. A black-and-white TV still works. It's functional. You can survive with it. But adding color changes everything. It makes the world of your experience brighter, more interesting, and ultimately so much more satisfying.

What's the difference between these two worlds of marriage? It all comes down to mindset: the subtle mental habits that shape how these two couples think, act, and interpret their partners' actions.

The 80/80 Mindset of Radical Generosity

Your mindset is the way you see the world. It includes your beliefs, thoughts, and attitude. It's like glasses you wear that shape your experience of marriage and life. When you see life through 80/20 glasses, you live in a world where the goal is to do your job, to fulfill your proper role as husband or wife. When you see life through 50/50 glasses, you live in a world of comparison, of constant scorekeeping and thus constant resentment and tension.

When you see life through 80/80 glasses, by contrast, the world changes. You're no longer stuck in the rigid gender roles of the 1950s. You're no longer looking at married life as a fair exchange of goods. Through this lens, your partner becomes a teammate, a friend, a lover, and a true partner in a bigger game where the goal isn't being right or making everything fair, but winning together.

This is the 80/80 mindset. It's a mindset that can appear like ordinary generosity. Generosity changes the atmosphere of marriage. It's doing more than you have to. It's contribution for its own sake. It's giving with no strings attached. Generosity flips the ordinary mindset of marriage upside down, from asking, "What have you done for me?" to asking, "What can I do for you?"

The goal of the 80/80 marriage is to push generosity to the extreme. That's why we call it *radical* generosity. Radical generosity isn't an occasional generous act. It isn't an idea you think about every now and then but rarely act on. Radical generosity is the extreme aspiration to do much more than your fair share and to turn this mindset into an ordinary way of being in a marriage. When you spend two weeks planning a surprise fortieth birthday for your partner, without any expectation of getting something in return, that's radical generosity. When you drive your partner back and forth from the hospital so they can spend time with a sick parent without asking why they've never driven you around, that's radical generosity. When you stop defending your side and "lose" an argument by saying, "I'm not sure what we're fighting about, but what I really want you to know is that I love you," that's radical generosity.

These generous actions break us out of the tit-for-tat calculus of fairness. They operate in a new and different world, one where you are more interested in supporting, helping, and loving your partner than in worrying about whether you're giving more than 50 percent or getting less than that in return. It's a contagious attitude that has the power to dissolve resentment and create a new world of marriage beyond 50/50.

The 80/80 Rule

We've come up with some simple math to help you make sense of this leap from fairness to radical generosity. It starts with blowing up the old calculations of marriage. We've already seen why the existing ratios of 80/20 and 50/50 break down. We've also seen that to break free of these deeply ingrained habits of mind, we need a new goal that's radical, even extreme. The goal is radical generosity. The ratio is 80/80. And the way we reach it is by using the 80/80 rule: I strive for 80 percent, you strive for 80 percent.

As we mentioned earlier, we're well aware that this ratio makes no sense—that a 160 percent whole is a mathematical impossibility. But marriage is beyond math. It's so much more. At its best, marriage takes us out of time and space. It's the joy of connection, the ecstasy of making love, and the support that comes from leaning on each other during hard times.

True, putting in 80 percent in your marriage may not make sense. It may feel uncomfortable. It may even shock your spouse when you manage to do it. But this extreme goal of striving for 80/80 might forever change your experience of marriage.

The Three Elements of Mindset

What does it look like to live the 80/80 rule—to stay in the mindset of radical generosity by giving 80 percent? The next three chapters will fill out the answer. As you will see, this 80 percent spirit of radical generosity reshapes our marriage mindset in three ways.

The first is contribution, or *what you do*. Radical generosity pushes us to contribute to the mundane tasks of ordinary life in a new and unexpected way. Contributing at 80 percent to housework, childcare, emotional labor, planning, logistics, and investing in the strength of your marriage means always trying to do more than your fair share. It's a mental habit that might seem insignificant but has profound benefits. As one man who had just emerged from a time of crisis told us, "We're getting annihilated by life. So if we're not purposeful, literally every day, about doing small things along the way that constantly build and acknowledge our relationship, everything starts to fall apart."

The second is appreciation, or *what you see*. Radical generosity pushes us to see the world of our marriage in a new way. Instead of scanning our partner's acts for moments when they messed up, dropped the ball, or did less than their fair share, we look at life through the lens of appreciation. When we spot them doing something right—helping out around the house or supporting the family—we tell them about it. These simple moments of appreciation can transform the experience of marriage. As a working mother of two young children told us, "To know that my spouse sees me and sees how hard I'm working, whether it's for the kids or for him, to be acknowledged for what I do—that re-fuels me."

The third is revealing, or *what you say*. Radical generosity pushes us from the safety of withholding our resentment, disappointment, and conflicts from our partner to revealing the full truth of our experience. In 80/20 and 50/50, it's easy to stay safe by avoiding the risk of revealing too much. It's also fair to hold back. If your partner isn't fully reveal-ing their issues, why should you? But radical generosity calls for some-thing different. It's a push to reveal your hard truths as a gift to the marriage, so that you can live together with less tension and resentment. One woman we interviewed told us, "We will actually say to each other, 'We've got to get clear.' Otherwise it affects every aspect of life. With-out these moments, I'm not a good mom, I'm not a good wife, and I'm not a good business owner."

When you begin to change your mindset in these three ways—when radical generosity informs what you do, see, and say—that's when you begin to uproot the old habits that keep you coming back to the resent-ment of 80/20 and 50/50 life. Radical generosity offers a path to a new mindset and a new, 80/80 experience of being together.

The 80/80 Rule in Practice

It's worth mentioning that just because you strive toward 80 percent doesn't mean you will always achieve it. As we learned in earlier chap-ters, because of our contribution blind spot, most of us have no idea when we're getting even close to doing our fair share. Instead, our ten-dency is to overestimate our own contributions and underestimate our partner's.

This means that shooting for 80 percent probably isn't going to result in you actually achieving it. But that's not a problem, because even if you never reach the goal, this new aspiration alone changes your mindset. Simply striving toward 80 percent rewires your thinking from tit-for-tat and quid pro quo to ideas that might have once seemed crazy: doing your partner's laundry, making dinner three times in a row, giving them a compliment in the car after they just criticized your lane-changing technique, or revealing your experience by telling them you felt upset when you weren't included in the planning for a family event.

You might also worry that this mindset isn't practical—that it's likely to break down the moment life gets crazy. But consider Mike. He has an extremely demanding job and two teenage kids, and he feels the constant strain of balancing work and family time. As he told us, "I'm busy. My wife is busy. And then there's the fact that we're surrounded by extended family that seems to be perpetually in crisis. We've got friends going through divorces. This stuff never stops. It's preposterous."

And yet just before our interview, Mike told us that he had ten spare minutes that he used to find his wife in the house, give her a huge kiss, and tell her, "I'm so grateful for the work you do for our family each day." This couple is deep in the thicket of busyness and stress. But as Mike told us, "These micro-moments of generosity create the connective tissue so that the busyness doesn't wreck it. Because of these moments, our connectedness stays intact no matter how busy we get."

The point here is that you don't have to be on vacation, feeling great, or living in a state of perfect balance to live in this mindset of radical generosity. It's a mindset you can experience anytime, anywhere—even during times of extreme stress, busyness, and crisis. In fact, you may find that radical generosity becomes even more powerful during these difficult times.

The Two Traps of Radical Generosity

At this point, some of you might be thinking, "Radical generosity sounds amazing, and if my partner were the Dalai Lama or even just more like the caring parent on a family sitcom, the 80/80 rule would work out great. But my spouse would never do this. So if I go all out with 80/80, it will end up being more like 80/20 in my partner's favor, and that sucks for me."

We've heard some version of this from countless people, most of them women. It's a response that brings to light two important barriers to the mindset of radical generosity.

Inequality Phobia

Striving for 80 percent is not just countercultural. In a world of 50/50 marriages, making this shift often results in no small amount of fear and anxiety. We're here to tell you that's actually a good sign—it means that you're doing it right.

Leaving the familiar ground of 50/50 contribution is like a journey into the psychological unknown. It sparks a uniquely modern condition that we call *inequality phobia*. The moment you go beyond 50 percent, you have to grapple with one of the most unpleasant thoughts of the 50/50 life: *I'm doing more than my spouse.* And for most of us, this thought immediately spawns a torrent of other thoughts: *Why am I doing more? Are they more important than me? Is their time more valuable than mine? Are they somehow better than me? Do they have more power than I do?*

This is the kind of mental tsunami that has the potential to rip apart even the most stable of marriages. So when these thoughts arise—and we can just about guarantee they will—your job is to stay cool. You may want to react, call out your spouse on how little they do, or desperately seek credit for your amazing contributions. But here again, see if you can just stay present in this uncomfortable place.

As you become more comfortable in the 80/80 space of radical generosity, you'll begin to notice something amazing. You'll see how this simple virtue dissolves your partner's resentment, opens their heart, and leads to deeper connection. You'll experience firsthand why generosity is the gateway to the deepest forms of love.

You might also notice that this ability to stay present with the discomfort of inequality phobia isn't just good for your marriage. It's a mindset that will also help you become more resilient in the rest of your life. By staying with, instead of checking out from, discomfort, you're increasing your threshold for stress, unpleasant emotions, and difficult conversations—a skill that will allow you to face all of life's challenges with greater ease.

The My-Partner-Would-Never-Do-This Problem

Now for a bigger problem. Many people, both women and men, but mostly women, see their partners as incapable of reciprocating this kind of 80/80 radical generosity. It's a sentiment expressed in phrases like "He's a lost cause," "She would never do that," and "He's got it so good with me doing everything that there's no reason for him to change."

And this begs the question: "Why should I be radically generous if my partner will never do the same for me?" If this feels like a burning question for you, now might be the time to jump ahead to chapter fourteen, "Resistance—The Reluctant Partner." This worry, after all, is likely to follow you throughout the book, and that's why we have an entire chapter dedicated to it, one that will help you see whether the 80/80 model is possible for you and your partner and that will push you to explore how you might be contributing to this dynamic.

If you want to keep moving ahead, however, then the short answer to this question is simply this: to break out of the fairness-based standoff of the 50/50 model, someone has to go first. Otherwise, you just stay caught in the stalemate—you and your partner both hold back, waiting for the other person to make the first move. It's an unproductive waiting game fueled by beliefs like "He's the one who should be radically generous—I'm doing just about everything to begin with," or "I already do 80 percent around the house and put in 80 percent in our marriage—there's no way I'm going to make an effort to be more generous."

You have two ways to respond to this kind of marital standoff. The first is to keep doing what you're doing, to stay caught in the grip of resentment or passive-aggressiveness toward your partner, to cling to your belief that your partner is incapable of radical generosity. This option will lead to a predictable outcome: everything will stay the same.

The second option is to try out this practice without ever even telling your partner that you're doing it, to see what happens when you bring radical generosity into your shared world. Because even though you might be doing more than your fair share now, chances are you're not doing it from a place of generosity. If you are like most people, you're likely doing these things out of obligation, resentment, or the fear that if you don't, no one else will.

By doing the acts you already do or adding small acts of kindness without this tit-for-tat motive of 50/50 fairness, you alone can quite possibly change the underlying culture of your marriage—you can ignite a contagious spirit of generosity that actually does have the power to get your partner more engaged in the relationship and may even make them more likely to be radically generous in return.

Just imagine what life would be like if you took this risk and it actually worked. Imagine a world where the mindset of your relationship flipped on its head, from "What you can do for me?" to "What I can do for you?" Imagine how much less you would fight. Imagine how much better you would feel. Imagine how much more you would love and appreciate your partner. It's a life-changing shift. And that's why we think it's worth giving radical generosity a try.

The Radical Generosity Shift

80/80
PRACTICE

Saying you want to be more radically generous is like saying you want to drink more water—it's helpful, but it doesn't answer an essential question: How? How can you shift to radical generosity when you're rushing to get out the door in the morning or feeling exhausted at the end of a marathon workday?

Here are two techniques.

The Easy Shift

This move is perfect for shifting from the ordinary experience of everyday life to this new mindset of radical generosity.

Move 1: Catch yourself (in 80/20 or 50/50).
Move 2: Think to yourself, "80/80" or "Radical generosity."

The first move is to notice when you're caught in the old mindset of 80/20 or 50/50. The second is to give yourself a subtle mental cue to shift by thinking "80/80" or "Radical generosity." Just planting this mental seed helps to redirect your attention to radical generosity.

The Hard Shift

Now for the more difficult move. This is the move from the state of stress, anger, or resentment to radical generosity. It's the "hard shift" because you're now switching from one side of the emotional spectrum to the other—from the depths of resentment to the heights of radical generosity.

Move 1: Catch yourself (in 80/20 or 50/50).
Move 2: Take three deep breaths.
Move 3: Think to yourself, "80/80" or "Radical generosity."

> The key difference is move two. When you're dysregulated by anger, irritation, or fear, it's essential to insert this short pause—to let these emotions move through and settle before taking the leap into radical generosity.

Now it's time to take radical generosity one step further—into what you do, what you see, and what you say in marriage.

CHAPTER 5

Contribution—What You Do

In 1994, Rob Israel, cofounder of Doc Popcorn, the world's largest franchise popcorn retailer, had a problem, but it wasn't about popcorn or business. Rob had a relationship problem.

He and his girlfriend of three years had just moved in together, and things weren't working out the way he had expected. When he returned from work one evening to an empty apartment, this background feeling of dissatisfaction grew, turning to anger. He sat on the couch that night, stewing in resentment, thinking to himself, *Why isn't she here? Why is this place such a mess? Why aren't we more connected, more intimate, and having more fun?*

As Rob's agitation escalated, he formed a mental plan of attack. He thought of all the things he wanted to say to her the moment she walked through the door. He thought of all the ways he wanted to blame her. But that's when Rob had what he described to us as a kind of "voice-of-God" moment. As if out of nowhere, a question popped into his mind:

"Well . . . what have you done for her?"

He sat. He reflected. And he felt stunned by this simple question. What surprised him most was that he didn't have a great answer. In fact, he couldn't even remember the last time he went out of his way to do something generous, something that would surprise and delight his girlfriend. He saw in that moment that he was expecting everything from her—love, support, intimacy, and connection—without giving much in return.

Inspired by this revelation, Rob left the apartment that night on a mission. He set out to surprise his girlfriend with a romantic dinner that included all her favorite things. He walked down the street from their apartment in New York City to her favorite Korean deli. He shopped for everything she loved. Then, as he was checking out at the cash register, his girlfriend walked through the door of the deli. The moment she realized Rob was there, buying all her favorite foods for a romantic late-night dinner, she melted.

It's a moment that changed the course of their relationship, opening up greater connection, love, and intimacy. As Rob told us, "I learned in that moment that I got everything I wanted by giving everything I wanted." He even developed a saying around this learning: "Do what you seek, get what you wish."

Rob's story is a story of contribution, the first of the three elements of radical generosity. His story reminds us that contributing in a radically generous way doesn't have to be outrageous, extraordinary, or expensive. You don't have to surprise your partner with a trip to Fiji, a new car, or concert tickets with backstage passes. In fact, some of the most powerful acts of contribution involve turning something ordinary, a morning breakfast or a late-night dinner, into an unexpected opportunity for generosity.

The *How* of Contribution

There are two sides to every act of contribution, both of which determine whether it lands as an act of love or a chit in the tit-for-tat game of fairness. There's *what* you do—the dinner you cook, the card you write, or the text you send. Then there's *how* you do it—the internal mindset that motivates the act.

It's tempting to think that *what* you do is the most important part of the contribution equation. And it's true that contributing in the right ways, with skillful actions, matters (more on that in the next section). But *how* you contribute—the mindset motivating you to act—has an even greater impact on the way these acts of contribution land for both partners.

To understand the power of mindset, consider the age-old marital to-do of washing dishes. This very same act of contribution can be done in one of three ways, each of which radically alters the atmosphere of marriage.

The first is the 80/20 way. You do the dishes because, chances are, you're the wife and *it's your job*. If you're the other partner, by contrast, you wander off to watch TV or read the evening paper. Why? Because doing dishes isn't your job. This leaves the dish-doer scrubbing crumbs and ketchup stains off a pile of plates with a mental attitude that goes something like "This is just what I have to do. It's my job."

The second is the 50/50 way. You do the dishes because *it's your turn*. You're not elbows-deep in dish soap because it's your job. Your partner, after all, is a 50/50 equal, so they could just as easily take on the task. You're washing the dishes either because it's your turn or because your partner totally blew it and didn't take their turn. Either way, you're left with a sponge in hand and a mindset that goes something like "Why am I doing the dishes again? It's the third day in a row," or "This isn't fair. Every time she cooks, she leaves me with three times as many dishes to clean," or "Thank goodness it's not my turn tomorrow."

The third is the 80/80 way. You do the dishes because *it's your gift*. The act of contribution is exactly the same as before. You're washing the dishes. But *how* you do it couldn't be more different. In this third world, washing the dishes isn't a domestic loan or a bargaining chip to cash in later. It's a living example of the 80/80 rule. It's a gift, an act of service given with no strings attached, with no expectation of getting something back in return.

Of course, you're only human, which means you might not be able to maintain this Gandhi-like dish-washing mindset all the time. But when you lose it, when you slip back into the 50/50 mindset of fairness, you catch yourself and return to radical generosity with thoughts like "My partner seems really stressed tonight. I wonder what else I can do to be supportive," or "We're on the same team here. My washing dishes helps both of us."

This shift in mindset has two powerful effects. First, it's contagious. Ordinary acts of contribution done from radical generosity soften the resentment of your partner. They're like ripples on a pond, spreading this spirit of radical generosity throughout the entire family system. As one man told us, "My wife and I have always tried to think, 'What can I do to help?' and when everyone has that attitude, it becomes contagious. Even the kids see it and feel inspired by it."

The second benefit of this shift in mindset is more personal. It transforms *your* experience of marriage. Even if your partner never notices you sweeping up the crumbs on the floor, paying the electric bill, or organizing playdates, your radically generous mindset changes *your* experience of these everyday acts. It dissolves the inner energy drain of resentment, replacing it with kindness and love.

The point here is that the power of contribution goes far beyond what you do. The real power of these acts arises from how you do it, from doing these acts with a mindset of radical generosity.

The *What* of Contribution

How you contribute sets the tone. But that doesn't mean what you do is irrelevant. If it really didn't matter, you could achieve marital bliss through generous but totally random acts of contribution: doing six a.m. cartwheels in the hallway, polishing every doorknob in the house, or painting the rocks in your driveway a Day-Glo shade of pink.

Some partners might love receiving these gifts. But most won't. And that's why the mindset of radical generosity is essential, but so is aligning your acts of contribution to the things that actually delight, surprise, or support your partner.

Think of this as understanding your partner's radical generosity map. This map tells you where to go and where not to go with your acts of contribution. It's essential to understand, because the very same acts that land with love and appreciation for one person may land with disgust and irritation for another.

Consider giving your partner a kiss on the forehead. One couple we spoke with told us this was the ultimate act of radical generosity. When the husband gave his wife a kiss there, she felt held, supported, and connected. But another woman told us that she felt patronized by a forehead kiss, like she was a child. As she explained, "I tell my husband that if he wants to kiss me on the forehead, he better be ready for a punch in the gut."

This is why understanding your partner's radical generosity map is so essential. It can be the difference between connection and frustration, or even between appreciation and a jab to the stomach.

How can you begin to better understand your partner's radical generosity map? How can your partner better understand yours? A good place to start is with the five primary areas of contribution outlined by author and marriage therapist Gary Chapman. As you read through this list, ask yourself: Which of these acts make me feel closer to my partner? Which have either no impact or perhaps even pull me away from connection?

- **Words of affirmation:** These are words of encouragement or appreciation. It's what happens when your partner gives you a compliment, a card, an "I love you" whispered into your ear, or a loving text message.
- **Quality time:** This is time spent together when your partner gives you their full, undivided attention. It's what happens when you go out on a date night, walk around your neighborhood, travel together, or even when you have a device-free meal together.

- **Receiving gifts:** Gifts don't have to be extravagant or cost tons of money. It's the thought that counts. It's what happens when you receive flowers, a box of chocolates, a drawing, a book, or even a unique stone that your partner found in the park.
- **Acts of service:** These are acts of contribution that help you relax, be supported, and feel seen. It's what happens when your partner services the car, walks the dog, folds laundry, drives the kids to baseball practice, or pulls out the clumps of hair clogging the shower drain.
- **Physical touch:** This is what happens when your partner reaches out to hold your hand, surprises you with a kiss, or gives you a huge morning hug or an unexpected back rub.[1]

Use this list to initiate a conversation with your partner. Once you identify and share the areas that lead you to deeper levels of connection, you'll both hold the secret to contribution. You can now combine the mindset of radical generosity (the how) with acts of contribution tailored to your partner's map of radical generosity (the what). That's the formula Rob used at the beginning of the chapter to surprise his girlfriend with her favorite dinner. It's the formula you can use at any time to shift from 50/50 to 80/80.

The 80/90 Nudge

In an ideal world, you and your partner would both take on this 80/80-style of contribution with equal enthusiasm. Most couples, however, don't live in that world. They live in a world of marriage where one person is sorting out how to renew the home and auto insurance while the other is sorting out whether to watch *American Idol* or *Monday Night Football*.

So it's worth considering: What do you do if contribution remains one-sided? What if one partner contributes far more than the other?

In many couples, after all, there's an over-contributing and an under-contributing partner, a partner who puts in more and a partner who puts in less. And as we've seen, when it comes to heterosexual couples, statistically speaking, women tend to play the role of over-contributor, while men play under-contributor.

These hard facts of our current cultural condition mean that the 80/80 spirit of contribution and radical generosity might need a bit of tweaking in some couples. And that's where the 80/90 Nudge comes in. If you are like most couples, it's likely that there's still work to be done in unwinding the inequality hangover from a few thousand years of unequal coupling. Hence the 80/90 Nudge: the over-contributing partner still shoots for 80 percent, but the under-contributing partner pushes their edge even further, to something more like 90 percent.

This nudge doesn't let the over-contributing partner (generally the woman) off the hook. They're still striving to move beyond 50 percent and build the mindset of radical generosity. But it's also a not-so-subtle reminder to the under-contributing partner to reach even further—to push so far toward radical generosity that they begin to close this gap.

Whether you're aspiring to contribute with a mindset of 80/80 or 80/90, the next step is to turn these radically generous acts of contribution into daily habits—to bring this 80/80 spirit into even the most mundane aspects of daily life.

Here's how to do it.

One Radically Generous Contribution a Day

80/80
PRACTICE

In this chapter, we're basically telling you to take generosity further than you ever have before. It's a strange aspiration. But it's also a life-changing one. So how can you shift the way you do ordinary acts of contribution to embody this radical, 80/80 mindset?

EACH DAY, DO ONE RADICALLY GENEROUS ACT OF CONTRIBUTION FOR YOUR PARTNER.

This doesn't mean buying your partner a Peloton or a weeklong trip to Aruba. These are ordinary acts of kindness that have the power to alter the entire atmosphere of marriage.

- Watch the kids early in the morning so your partner can sleep in.
- Restock the fridge.
- Plan a surprise date night.
- Leave a love letter on his or her pillow.
- Give your partner a five-minute shoulder massage.
- Give your partner time to see an old friend.
- Toast your partner at the beginning of dinner for his or her work at home or at the office.

Tip: Make your contributions count

Don't forget the key insight around the radical generosity map: choose something that matches your partner's language of contribution.

Want a More Advanced Practice?

WHEN YOU DO THIS GENEROUS ACT, DO IT WITHOUT SEEKING CREDIT.

There's a part of all of us that craves approval, attention, and credit for all our amazing deeds. The advanced radical generosity practice is to act from generosity while simultaneously letting go of this credit-seeking instinct. Watch yourself squirm and see what it's like to do something generous without ever being noticed or thanked. Here are some examples:

- Restock the fridge (while your partner isn't there and without announcing your kind act when they return).

- Plan a surprise date night (and don't tell your partner how hard it was to plan or how long it took you).
- Fill up their car with gas (without telling them you did it).
- You get the idea.

As we have seen, these simple acts will help you feel happier, less resentful, and more connected, while doing the same for your partner. And that's how you enter the upward spiral of generosity. That's the first step in shifting from the conflict-ridden world of 50/50 to this new, more alive, 80/80 world.

CHAPTER 6

Appreciation—What You See

It's eight thirty on a Thursday night. Amy is returning home from a rare night out with her friends at a local restaurant. She walks through the door and enters a scene of total domestic anarchy. Her husband and her two kids have turned the living room couch into a massive blanket fort. Greasy pizza boxes and dirty plates litter the kitchen sink and counters. Pirate costumes and princess dresses are scattered about the floor.

As she almost trips over a toy school bus in the hallway, Amy feels a wave of rage. This whole crazy scene is yet another reminder of her husband Mike's inability to clean up after himself and his pattern of being irresponsible. If she's honest with herself, tinges of jealousy also stoke the flames of resentment. *Why does he get to be the fun one? Why can't I have a night like this, where I get to go crazy with the kids and have someone else clean up after me?* she thinks.

And that's why, after picking up the mess, once the kids are asleep later that night, she lays into Mike: "I leave the house for three hours and you destroy it. It's not fair."

It's ten thirty the next morning, across town. Eleanor is returning home from an early morning workout at her local yoga studio with a friend. She walks through the door and encounters a similar scene of domestic disarray. The blanket fort, the dirty dishes, and the costumes strewn all over the floor. Her husband, Steve, and her kids have clearly had an amazing time while somehow managing to turn the entire house into a complete mess.

Like Amy, part of Eleanor feels an immediate surge of anger. But another part experiences something quite different. She feels grateful. Grateful to have a husband willing to watch her kids while she does yoga on a Sunday morning. Grateful that while they may have trashed the place, they clearly had fun.

So, seconds after walking through the door, Eleanor says, "Oh my gosh. It looks like you have had a blast! How about we turn the cleanup effort into a game so we can go out to the park this afternoon?" Later that night, as she and her husband lie in bed, she tells him, "I love how you bring fun and adventure to our kids' lives." She also tells him, "It would mean a lot to me if you and the kids picked up before I got home next time."

Amy and Eleanor returned home to the same chaotic scene. And yet their reactions couldn't have been more different. Amy viewed this scene through the 50/50 lens of fairness. For her, this mess served as yet another reminder of her husband's inability to manage himself, let alone their two kids. Eleanor viewed this same scene through the 80/80 lens of radical generosity. For her, this mess served as a reminder of her husband's uncanny ability to bring a spirit of play and exploration to her children.

So why does Amy see problems where Eleanor sees reasons for appreciation? It all comes back to mindset. Each of these women sees the world of her marriage through a radically different lens, which shapes her interpretation of everything her husband says, does, or, more important, doesn't do.

That's the power of mindset. It sounds subtle, but what you choose to see in your marriage colors your experience of your life together. It has the power to turn every waking moment into a relentless stream of reasons to feel angry, resentful, or disappointed. But it also has the power to turn every moment into an opportunity to see the unique strengths, insights, and contributions of your partner.

This is the second element of the radical generosity mindset: what you see. It's what happens when we push beyond our ordinary way of seeing our partner, when we see them from the perspective of radical generosity. It's the practice of appreciation.

The Science of Appreciation in Marriage

Why is changing what you see so powerful? John Gottman, the world's leading researcher on the science of marriage, has spent decades exploring this question. He has, in fact, turned the seemingly ethereal art of love and generosity into a cold, hard science, using what his team calls the Love Lab.

Gottman's Love Lab turns ordinary couples into marital lab rats. They record couples hashing out their differences over money, sex, or housework, all while strapped to sensors and electrodes.[1] This may sound like some sort of psychotic reality show, but it helped shed light on a question that has perplexed marriage researchers for years: Why do some couples thrive while others struggle to survive? Or in Gottman's terms, why are some couples masters and others disasters?[2]

The answer, drawn from thirty years of extensive research, boils down to what we witnessed in Amy and Eleanor: happy couples see things differently. According to Gottman, "There's a habit of mind that the masters have, which is this: they are scanning the social environment for things they can appreciate and say thank you for. They're building this culture of respect and appreciation very purposefully."[3] Happy couples, in other words, see the world of their marriage through this lens of appreciation.

Gottman has even translated this skill of marriage masters into a simple formula: 5 to 1. Marriages that thrive experience five positive interactions for every one negative interaction. For every criticism, insult, or complaint, in other words, these couples express five compliments, appreciations, kisses, or gentle touches. Some couples take this even further. They're like marriage Olympians, interacting with something like a 20-to-1 ratio of positive to negative interactions.[4]

Unhappy couples, by contrast, see their partners differently. They're not looking for things to appreciate in each other. They're scanning each moment to catch their partner screwing up. And when that happens—when their partner walks in the door late, forgets to pick up milk on the way home, or doesn't follow through—they're ready to berate them with criticism, passive-aggressiveness, or ridicule.

And that's why Gottman claims the uncanny ability to predict with over 90 percent accuracy whether a couple will get divorced.[5] It doesn't matter what they're fighting about. It doesn't matter how often they have sex. It doesn't even matter whether they are rich or poor. What matters is this invisible atmosphere of interaction. If the couple bounces back from conflict by redirecting their attention to appreciation and love, they're going to make it. If they get stuck in a swirl of criticism, withdrawal, and indifference, they're destined for divorce or a lifetime of chronic unhappiness.

The Prehistoric Threat to Appreciation

So why haven't we all made this shift to seeing marriage through the lens of appreciation? Why do the vast majority of couples see their partner's every move through a far more negative lens? Why do we seem to default to criticism and judgment, rather than gratitude and appreciation?

The problem isn't that we're intentionally immature, petty, or ungrateful. The problem is that we're wired to be this way.

Over the past thirty years, neuroscientists and evolutionary psychologists have come to realize that the human brain isn't wired to see life through the positive lens of appreciation. It's wired to fixate on the negative—to experience life with a far more pessimistic mindset of vigilance and anxiety. It's a mental quirk that researchers call the *negativity bias*.[6]

The reason for this adaptive trait is relatively straightforward. In primitive times, when we were hunting for food on the savannah with sharpened rocks and stone axes, living in a state of constant anxiety was far more advantageous than living in the bliss of gratitude and appreciation.

Sure, it might be nice to appreciate your partner for making you that new animal skin cape to keep you warm in the winter. But staying on guard and anxious, scanning your environment for potential threats, is what kept you alive. It's the mindset that helped you stay alert to the saber-toothed tiger lurking behind those bushes, the poisonous snake slithering into your cave, or the looming drought that threatened to wipe out your entire village.

We complain about a lot of things these days: feeling pressed for time, working at all hours, and having to witness everyone else's magical moments on social media. But we have the unprecedented luxury of worrying about all sorts of things that pose almost no risk to our basic survival, things like why our partner can't seem to load the dishwasher right or why they're never in the mood after watching *Dancing with the Stars* on a Wednesday night.

This is the paradox of being human in our modern age. Our culture, technology, and the very institution of marriage itself have changed at warp speed over the past six thousand or so years. Our brains, however, haven't changed much at all. They're still wired for prehistoric days.

That's what makes living with a mindset of appreciation so hard. We're working against our own neurobiology. We're constantly confronted by the fact that our default state is to see the messes in life as a threat, like Amy did at the beginning of the chapter. And even though nobody has ever died because of the collapse of a living-room blanket fort, our bodies respond to these kinds of domestic threats with a similar flood of stress hormones, which isn't just bad for our marriages. It's also a key cause of stress-related health conditions such as diabetes, anxiety, depression, and cognitive degeneration.[7]

Evolutionary psychology helps explain why even though we may know the benefits of appreciation, even though we may be convinced that Gottman's 5-to-1 ratio is the path to a better married life, our biology exerts a constant pull in the other direction.

That's the bad news.

The good news is that these facts about our wiring also help point us toward the way out. They give us the clues to how we can create a new way of seeing the world of marriage from the mindset of appreciation.

How to See Appreciation

Because we're all working against our own biology, it's not enough to express appreciation when inspiration strikes. You can't just wait for it to happen. You have to make it happen. In short, the way to reverse the momentum of our biology is through building the skill of appreciation the same way you might develop any other habit, such as flossing your teeth, volunteering once a month at your local homeless shelter, or going to a six a.m. Pilates class three times a week.

It's the same way we approach contribution. The goal is to turn this new way of seeing marriage into a regular habit, something that happens almost automatically. When we do, it turns out that these two habits actually work together, much like call-and-response, an age-old technique used in classical, blues, jazz, and popular music. Take, for example, the Beatles' "With a Little Help from My Friends." When they all sing, "Do you need anybody?" that is the call. When Ringo Starr sings, "I just need someone to love," that is the response.

Happy couples do the very same thing. When one person offers a compliment at dinner, leaves a card on the bedside table, or sends a heartfelt text message, that is the call. That's one of those magic moments of radically generous contribution. It's an act driven by the desire to give but also begging for some sort of response.

Appreciation is the response. It's how we make music in marriage. When one partner makes the bed, takes care of a sick child, or goes out of their way for the other, appreciation is seeing and acknowledging these contributions. It's saying to your partner, "I see you. I see how generous you are. I see how much you are trying. And I value how much you care."

Marriage without appreciation is like a call with no response. As one man told us, "With summer coming up and camps filling up, I spent the last two weeks going online and booking camps for the entire summer for our two boys. And I'm still waiting on a thank-you. It's a little thing, but it matters to me." These are the sounds of a call with no response, the sounds of contribution going unseen and unappreciated.

So contribution and appreciation go together. When both become daily rituals in your house, they feed off each other. They create a new atmosphere of connection, a new, radically generous, 80/80 mindset.

The Challenge and Power of Living in an Appreciation Mindset

As you begin building this habit of seeing life through the lens of appreciation, you may bump up against a common challenge: forgetting to do it. Life gets crazy, your kid throws up in the backseat of the car, your babysitter cancels the night before a school holiday to go on a last-minute camping trip, or you discover a new species of mold living in your basement. When these things happen, you can quickly forget all about generosity and appreciation.

To overcome this challenge, it can be helpful to leverage the science of habit formation by setting up a regular cue—a reminder that helps you actually remember to express appreciation. One couple we spoke with, for instance, uses dinner as their cue. They start the meal by expressing appreciation for each other. For other couples, the time just before going to sleep, when they are lying in bed recapping the day, is the perfect time. This cue works like a life alarm clock (more on that in chapter fifteen). It's your regular reminder to continue building the mindset of appreciation.

Why put in the work to build this new habit? Many couples told us that the reward makes all the effort worth it. Take Saurab and Anjani. In the early days of their marriage, Saurab observed, "I used to say that in a marriage that is deep and strong, you never need to say thank you. But if I'm honest with myself, I now think that if I've gone out of my way to do something, a thank-you means a lot. Because I have an ego and, like all human beings, that expression of appreciation validates what I did—whether it's a date, a moment, or something I've said. It means something. It matters."

His wife, Anjani, agrees. As she told us, "To know that he sees me and sees how hard I'm working is so important. It refuels me. We get caught up in doing all sorts of things, but when he sees me and appreciates me, it feels like we're holding hands again."

In fact, the more we talked to couples, the more we noticed a pattern. Appreciation and criticism work like deposits and withdrawals from a bank account. Thanking your partner for planning a trip—that's a deposit in the emotional bank. Appreciating your partner in front of your family for cooking an amazing meal—that's more money in the bank.

Telling your partner that the way they eat is annoying—that's a small withdrawal. Suggesting that your partner hit the gym a few more times each week to slim down their dad bod—that's another withdrawal. Insulting your partner's intelligence in front of friends at a dinner party— that's the kind of withdrawal that brings you close to a zero balance.

The point is that appreciation and criticism work to either build or destroy your relationship's net worth. If you live with a mindset of criticism, indifference, and contempt, the data says you're likely to become relationally destitute. But whether you're financially rich or poor, if you can build the habit of seeing your marriage through the lens of appreciation, you become relationally rich. And over time, the surplus in your account grows so large that when the tough times come, as they always do, your relationship surplus gives you a cushion to fall back on. That's the power of appreciation.

So just as you started building the habit of one generous contribution a day in the previous chapter, you'll now begin building its response, the habit of one appreciation a day.

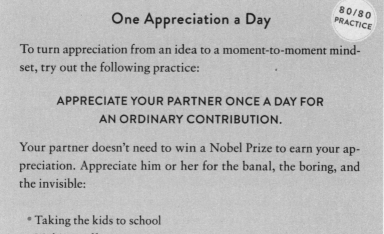

One Appreciation a Day

80/80 PRACTICE

To turn appreciation from an idea to a moment-to-moment mindset, try out the following practice:

APPRECIATE YOUR PARTNER ONCE A DAY FOR AN ORDINARY CONTRIBUTION.

Your partner doesn't need to win a Nobel Prize to earn your appreciation. Appreciate him or her for the banal, the boring, and the invisible:

- Taking the kids to school
- Making coffee
- Wiping down the counters
- Researching an upcoming trip
- Thinking ahead to plan a date night
- Reaching out to friends to set up a dinner

Tip: Make it your own

This doesn't have to be forced, scripted, and formal. Make it funny, unexpected, or quirky. Make the way you express appreciation authentic to you. For some people, it sounds like "Thank you for bringing me coffee." For others, it might sound like "When you brought me that cup of coffee, I could really feel how much you care about me." For others, it might sound like "You are the man! Coffee in bed at six thirty. I love it!" The content may change but the form is the same. It's a simple recognition of your partner's contributions.

Want a More Advanced Practice?

Notice those times when you feel unappreciated by your partner. Notice when you worked hard on planning something, hosting an event, or cleaning out the garage and your partner didn't even notice (at least in your mind). When this happens, here's your practice:

ASK YOUR PARTNER FOR APPRECIATION.

We know what you're thinking: "Are you crazy? That's on them. I can't ask for appreciation." But even the most in-tune partners miss things, and more oblivious partners need help remembering the practice of appreciation. When it comes to appreciation, as with all things in a relationship, it's all right to ask for what you want. This doesn't have to be a big deal. It's as easy as saying, "I worked really hard planning this trip, and I notice that I want to be appreciated by you," or "I know we're all doing our share, but I spent a long time cleaning up the kitchen today and I'd love a comment or a thanks."

CHAPTER 7

Revealing—What You Say

Mark and Jill weren't some naive and uninformed couple when it came to marriage. They were marriage experts. Mark had spent twenty years working as the family life pastor at a megachurch. Together with Jill, he created a successful marriage ministry that helped everyone from newlyweds to couples on the verge of divorce learn what they called the "ABC's of a healthy marriage."

They didn't just teach and preach this stuff. They lived it. As Jill told us, "We were doing a lot of the right things on the outside. We were doing date nights. We would go on trips, just the two of us. We knew each other's love languages and we spoke them regularly."

So you can imagine the panic and disbelief when Jill found Mark asleep in bed one night with his phone in his hand and noticed a text conversation on the screen confirming her worst fear: Mark was having an affair.

In that moment, Mark and Jill's life changed forever. Weeks later, Mark moved out of the house, intent on pursuing the woman on the other side of that text conversation. Jill spent the next several months in extreme emotional distress.

In the end, they decided to try to make things work, an effort that involved years of soul-searching and intensive couples therapy. And yet even as they searched for answers, they couldn't seem to come up with a clear explanation for Mark's affair. Unlike with other stories of infidelity, there wasn't a clear reason—no radical life change, layoff at work, tragic death, or life-changing diagnosis. It just kind of happened.

After two years of carefully examining the invisible emotional undercurrents that had led to Mark's affair, they never did find a single cause. Instead, they found hundreds, if not thousands, of small moments of disconnection that metastasized over time like a marital cancer. As Jill observed, "Looking back, it wasn't the big things that made a difference. It was the little things. Things that simmer under the surface. Things unnoticed. Unattended. Undetected. Untouched."[1]

After years of searching, they discovered that if anything caused the affair, it was these little issues that grew into bigger issues with time. As Mark told us, "Out of all this struggle, we learned a principle that we call *slow fades*. We started to see that these slow fades were always there, eroding the foundation of our marriage." *Slow fades* is Mark and Jill's phrase for the small ruptures in connection that gather over years or even decades. This insight led them to change their marriage by cleaning up all these tiny slow fades and to bring their story to the world in their book, *No More Perfect Marriages*.[2]

What we learn from Mark and Jill is that taken by themselves, none of these minor disruptions in connection really matter. Each disagreement, disappointment, or issue has almost no impact on the health of your marriage. But when thousands of these issues accumulate over time, the impact can be catastrophic. As Jill observed, "When your hearts are getting pulled apart a quarter inch at a time, you don't feel the quarter inch. But when a quarter inch is matched up with another quarter and another quarter and another quarter, you get to inches, and then feet and then miles apart."

The Momentum of Radical Generosity in Marriage

Mark and Jill remind us that there is no such thing as perfection in marriage. It's a point that sounds obvious, but it's easily forgotten. When you scan social media, you're rarely reminded of this fact. Instead, you're generally left with the opposite impression—that everyone else is living in some marital utopia filled with smiling anniversary-dinner photos, epic vacations, and date-night surprises.

The same is true of real life. When you watch that beautiful, fit, successful couple walk into a restaurant, all you see is the appearance of marital bliss. You don't get to see the fight that happened ten minutes earlier in the Uber on the way to the restaurant. You don't see the years they've spent in couples therapy desperately trying to avoid getting a divorce. You just see the smiles, the glow, and the facade that everything is amazing.

The 80/80 marriage model can fall into this same trap. Radical generosity can start to sound like some sort of marital paradise, a fantasy land where everyone always contributes at 80 percent and lavishes their partners with praise and appreciation. In truth, that world never has existed and likely never will. Even couples who live and breathe the 80/80 mindset still have bad days. They still snap at each other. They still feel pissed when the other person doesn't thank them. They still get caught in the trap of 80/20 deference and control or 50/50 fairness.

When this happens, it doesn't always work to just contribute more or appreciate your way back to connection. Sometimes you just have to say that things aren't working. Sometimes, the only way to get back on track is to let your partner know when you're hurt, upset, or frustrated. As one woman told us, "When it gets to a point where things get out of balance, where something is off, just communicating the frustration helps."

This move is the final part of the radical generosity mindset. It's what you say when the music of call-and-response—contribution and appreciation—starts to sound like karaoke night at the local bar. It's the practice of revealing. It's a way of being radically generous by revealing even the most seemingly insignificant fears, hurt feelings, and disappointments.

Like contribution and appreciation, it's a practice that's all about pushing your edge. Only this time, you're pushing an emotional edge. You're pushing beyond your comfort zone by telling your partner about the full range of your experience, both the good and the bad.

Revealing isn't always easy. But it's a powerful tool for clearing away unnecessary friction in the system of marriage. It's the ten-second "I'm sorry, babe, that came out wrong" apology after a sharp comment. It's revealing, "It matters to me that you come home from work on time for family dinner." It's saying, "I know this sounds nitpicky and crazy, but can you please try to stop leaving empty drinking glasses all over our bathroom counter?"

Couples who thrive have a way of quickly revealing this kind of everyday marital drama and getting back in sync. The couples who struggle often do the opposite. They let what Gay and Katie Hendricks call the "microscopic truths" of marriage go unspoken for weeks, months, years, or even decades.[3] And as we've seen, this failure to clear up the issues that arise often leads to a slow process of growing further apart.

Of course, communication has always been important in marriage. And yet, as sociologist and marriage researcher Daniel L. Carlson told us, with the shift away from the traditional 80/20 model to equality in marriage, it's now more important than ever. As he observed, "With egalitarian relationships, there's no road map. And so you have to talk. If you're not constantly communicating, organizing, and arranging things, the other person might forget to do something, and you now feel things are unfair because you're not talking about it with each other."

In fact, Carlson's latest research shows that communication is the key to equal marriage and shared responsibility. For men in particular, strong communication leads to a greater willingness to share housework, which in turn leads to greater marriage satisfaction and even better, more frequent sex.[4]

The Potholes and Sinkholes of Marriage

This practice of revealing and sex have one thing in common: they both involve the exchange of explosive emotional energy. If done skillfully, both activities can open up outrageous amounts of love and connection. If done unskillfully, both can tear a relationship apart, leaving behind a trail of bitterness, hurt feelings, and resentment.

When it comes to revealing, the explosiveness stems from the fact that we're expressing some of the most sensitive feelings in married life: disappointment, anger, and sadness. So if something goes wrong in the exchange, the risks are high. Things can easily spiral out of control, making the original issue worse, not better.

This means that before we reveal, we have to ask: How big an issue are we dealing with? Is this an emotional rain shower or a category five hurricane? We have to ask this question because the answer helps determine the best path forward to revealing our experience. As we will see, some problems are easy to solve with a simple reveal and request. Others create so much drama that they're almost impossible to solve on your own. Some problems, in other words, are potholes in the road of marriage; others are sinkholes.

Potholes

Potholes are the low-grade sources of friction in relationships that are annoying but tolerable. They're what Mark and Jill called slow fades. These aren't the big fights about parenting philosophy, sex, money, or feeling controlled. These are the smaller but more frequent tiffs over trivial stuff such as feeling unappreciated after planning a vacation, bickering over which set of friends to see on the weekend, or saying you're fine instead of asking your partner for what you really want.

These kinds of relational potholes may be annoying, but with honest conversation, many of them are fixable. Resolving a disagreement over where to send your kid to kindergarten—that's a fixable problem that goes away once your kid starts school. Fighting over whose job it should be to Swiffer the kitchen floor—also fixable. It's over as soon as you express your frustration and come up with a schedule for who cleans, or when you hire a housecleaning service to come every few weeks.

Even when these pothole problems aren't fixable, when the same ones keep coming back, they are at least manageable. If you communicate clearly about feeling disconnected when your partner works late at night after the kids go down, that's a manageable problem. If you can talk about feeling like you don't want to initiate sex because it seems your partner almost always says no, that's another manageable problem (more on sex in chapter thirteen).

The big idea here is that most of the everyday issues that pull us apart are either fixable or manageable, if—and this is a big *if*—we're willing to communicate clearly about these issues as they arise.

When it comes to these pothole problems, there's a tool you can use to reveal your experience and get back into connection with your partner. It's the practice we call Reveal and Request.

Reveal and Request

80/80 PRACTICE

When issues come up in marriage, we recommend this simple, time-efficient tool for resolving conflict called Reveal and Request. Here's how it works.

Step 1: Notice when you and your partner are out of sync

Here's how you know this is happening:

* You feel resentful toward your partner.
* You're thinking things aren't fair.

- You're cycling in your mind through past injustices committed by your partner.
- You pick a fight with your partner over something meaningless.
- You blame your partner for something out of his or her control (like rain during your vacation).

Simply becoming aware of falling out of sync is a monumental accomplishment. It gives you the ability to choose what to do next—to either pretend the issue doesn't exist (not recommended) or reveal it so you can get back into connection (a better choice).

Step 2: Reveal the issue

You can do this by expressing a Reveal and Request.

Reveal

Share your inner emotional experience:

- "I felt sad when . . ."
- "I felt angry when . . ."
- "It hurt my feelings when . . ."
- Or "I felt unappreciated when . . ."

This is just about revealing the inner experience keeping you from feeling connected.

Request

Tell your partner what he or she can do to get back into connection with you:

- "My ask is that you show up on time next week."
- "It's important to me that you follow through the next time you say you've got something handled."
- "Please don't call me by that name anymore."

Reveal and Request

Here's what it looks like when you combine these two:

- "I felt sad that you never thanked me for the work I did to finish our taxes [the reveal]. Next time I complete a big project for us, it's important to me that you say thanks [the request]."
- "I know you were joking, but it really hurt my feelings when you called me an idiot at dinner the other night [the reveal]. Can you please not call me that [the request]?"
- "I feel angry when you turn away from me after sex [the reveal]. Can you hold me for a few minutes before we go to sleep [the request]?"

Tip 1: Leverage the power of revealing while walking

"The most mind-expanding and considerate conversations," one woman we interviewed told us, "happen when we're walking together." The research of Harvard evolutionary biologist Christine Webb helps explain why. Her studies on conflict resolution show that walking during a tense conversation not only decreases stress but also increases positive rapport, empathy, and creative thinking.[5] So you might find that it's easier to reveal these issues on a walk.

Tip 2: Reveal the issue from a spirit of radical generosity

The motivation behind your Reveal and Request will determine how it lands for your partner. Anger triggers anger. Resentment triggers resentment. And radical generosity does the same. It triggers love, connection, and kindness. That's why the key to an effective Reveal and Request is to do it from this mindset of radical generosity.

What happens after a Reveal and Request? Now the ball is in the other partner's court, and there are really only two ways to respond: one that fixes the pothole and one that opens it up like a jackhammer.

The first response is driven by radical generosity. It's an acknowledgment of your partner's experience. It's saying something like "Wow, I can totally see how that would upset you." When it comes to your partner's request, your job as the listener is to respond with a kind and honest answer, which might sound like "Yes, I can do a better job of that next time," or might in some cases sound like "No, I want to help here but I can't commit to that."

The second, more problematic response is driven by fear, anger, or frustration. It sounds something like "Are you kidding me? If anyone should feel pissed off right now, it's me." This kind of response is a bad idea for so many reasons: It's not affirming. It's an attack. You have also signaled to your partner that it's not safe to be emotionally vulnerable with you—that they're better off withholding their true feelings.

Sinkholes

In contrast to the low-grade sources of friction we call potholes, you may also encounter bigger, less workable problems in marriage—sinkholes. Sinkholes are the issues that have become so explosive over time that they trigger an immediate surge of anger, irritation, fear, and the associated cocktail of stress hormones. Hitting a sinkhole in marriage is the same as driving into one on the road. It rarely ends well, and the more we try to pull ourselves out of it, the more we seem to just make it worse.

While potholes are fixable, or at least manageable, through conversation and revealing, sinkholes are so deeply rooted and so complex that we often can't navigate them alone. It's also worth remembering that even the most benign pothole problems can turn into massive sinkholes when we ignore them over long stretches of time.

The divide between these two kinds of problems can also become blurry. Some problems sit between these two extremes, triggering intense anger but not quite rising to the level of sinkhole conflicts. These problems fall short of posing an existential threat to the relationship, and the couples experiencing them have the tools to talk through them.

It's also worth noting that some couples get lucky. Their conflicts mostly arise as manageable pothole problems. They've never encountered an issue that has the potential to pry apart the foundation of their marriage.

When these sinkhole problems do arise, they can take a variety of forms.

There's the partner who feels lost and without a clear sense of purpose. He keeps saying yes to everything—kids, major life decisions, and a career in which he's just going through the motions. As a result, he feels like his partner is dragging him along through life, and he resents her for it.

There's the couple dealing with addiction. One partner continues to fall into the trap of drugs and alcohol, while the other keeps playing the role of rescuer, wondering how to put an end to this cycle of recovery and relapse.

There are couples struggling to figure out whether and how to rebuild their marriage after one partner cheated and the other feels betrayed, wondering whether they can ever trust each other again.

And then there's the couple who wants an equal marriage but keeps getting caught in a pattern in which one person does whatever they want—trips with friends, long naps, and Netflix binges—while the other does all the work around the house, manages all the logistics, and lives in a continuous state of resentment.

While revealing is a powerful tool for dealing with the potholes in married life, it can make things worse when dealing with sinkholes. When you hit a sinkhole as a couple, it's often essential to get help from outside the marital system. It could be a couples therapist. It could be a pastor or a rabbi. It could be a coach. But solving these complicated problems often requires someone outside your relationship who can give you a broader perspective and help you find your way back to stable ground.

Here's one last suggestion for dealing with potholes and sinkholes: take time to do your own personal work. You can build your emotional fitness through mindfulness practice, questioning your thoughts, better understanding your personality type, or developing your emotional intelligence. These strategies allow you to navigate more skillfully the surge of anger and fear that comes from misunderstanding and conflict. They make you calmer, less reactive, and simply better at having difficult conversations with your partner. This book isn't about developing these individual skills, but such development happens to be the central focus of much of our work with individuals and corporate clients. For our list of key tools for building these skills of mental and emotional resilience, check out the resources in the appendix.

You now have the tools to understand and practice radical generosity. This new mindset represents a fundamental shift in what you do, see, and say in marriage. The next step is to explore the structure of your life—things like roles, priorities, boundaries, power, and sex—and to unite this mindset of radical generosity with a structure of shared success.

PART 3

Building
a New Structure

CHAPTER 8

Shared Success—The 80/80 Structure

Whoa—When it comes to marriage, half the game is about mindset. As we have seen, it's about changing the inner experience of sharing a life together. It's about focusing less on fairness and more on radical generosity, on what we do, see, and say.

But what about the structures of marriage that live outside our minds? What about all the logistics, planning, roles, and priorities that go into sharing complicated lives together, in this complicated time, with another complicated human being?

You need more than just a generous mindset to navigate these external forces. You also need a *structure* designed to help you take on the messy task of sharing a life. In the 80/20 model, rigid gender roles shape the structure of life. In the 50/50 model, the structure becomes increasingly confused and chaotic. We lose clarity and a common purpose. We become two separate individuals, sometimes caught in subtle forms of competition, envy, and resentment, desperately trying to make things fair.

In the 80/80 marriage, the structure of life is yet again about pushing the edge of our ordinary habits in marriage. Only this time, we're pushing the edge of individual success and ambition. We're pushing against our cultural hardwiring that says each person should chase their dreams (alone) or that we're foolish not to look out for number one. The 80/80 model is based on an alternative goal for the way we structure life: shared success.

Two Worlds, Two Structures, Two Ways of Doing Marriage

What does individual and shared success look like in marriage? Just consider the words of two men reflecting on how they react when their partner experiences a win in their life or career.

RELATIONSHIP 1

We both have these crazy dreams. We want to accomplish so much, and we're both going for it. And we are supportive of each other. But let's say that she gets a huge job, and I don't, and my career isn't going as well as hers. I should be really happy for her. But I'm actually jealous because she just got something that I wanted. And I'll say, "Oh that's great, honey, wonderful!" But in my mind, I'm thinking, "Shit, now she's going to take off in her career and leave me behind."

RELATIONSHIP 2

One of the main reasons marriage has worked for us is that we always approach our careers not as hers and mine but as two parts of a whole. We've gone through different times where one of us has had to "compromise" their opportunity in order to allow the other person to pursue the greater opportunity between the two of us. That's never been a problem. Each of us has been in that position. Each of us has done it gladly to support the other. We've never really worried about who was making more money or who was more

successful. We don't think about it that way. We think, "What's the
bigger opportunity between the two of us?"

Imagine life in the first relationship. Your partner just got that big
promotion, closed a huge deal, or got elected president of the PTO. What
would it be like to hear that news and then immediately feel the sting
of envy? You're excited—how could you not be?—but you mostly feel
small and scared, comparatively worse off because of your partner's
success.

Now imagine hearing that same news from the second perspective.
Your family just had a huge day. Your partner won and so did you. It's
like being on a basketball team and watching your teammate sink the
game-winning three-pointer. Sure, your partner made the shot, but you
both won the game.

The difference between these relationships is the difference between
living in a world defined by fairness and individual achievement and living in a world defined by the spirit of winning together. The first world
reflects a structure in which each partner's career and much of their
lives are radically separate. The second reflects the world of shared
success—a structure of life that emphasizes "we" instead of "I," where
we strive for shared wins instead of individual victories.

The Five Elements of Structure

If radical generosity is the mental game of the 80/80 marriage, shared
success is the practical game of life logistics. It's the blueprint for organizing the tasks, to-dos, and decisions in married life around this radical goal of winning together. And yet it's not enough to just say, "All
right, let's work together." To make this shift real, we need to explore
how this new goal applies to the five areas of marriage where we're most
likely to get stuck: roles, priorities, boundaries, power, and sex.

We will explore each of these in depth in the coming chapters. But here's the short version of what happens when we integrate the goal of shared success with these five areas. Roles no longer arise from random historical accident but are designed around how we win together. Priorities are determined by a shared set of values. Boundaries become a way of saying no to the opportunities, requests, and demands of modern life that don't lead to shared success. Power becomes more balanced. And when it comes to sex, the most intimate domain of marriage, we encounter a surprising truth: the better the structure of shared success in marriage, the better the sex.

Marriage as a Team Sport

In our interviews with happy couples, we heard a common metaphor again and again: an 80/80 marriage is a "team sport." As one man told us, "For us, marriage is identical to being on a basketball team. If one of us isn't good at three-pointers, then that person focuses on passing. It's a team mindset that's the opposite of give-and-take. It's a mindset that says, 'What do we need to do together to win?'"

This idea of winning as a team may sound almost cliché. But living this way, in the midst of all the pressures of modern life, is a radical practice. It's an extreme departure from the structure of most marriages. The 80/20 way, after all, is like playing on a team where, yes, you both want to win, but only one player gets to take the shots. The 50/50 way, in contrast, is like playing on a team of all-stars, where both players are more concerned with driving up their individual stats and winning MVP than winning the overall game. The 80/80 way is about becoming a true team. It's about playing to each other's strengths, balancing power, and taking turns in the spotlight.

There's one other reason to take seriously this team metaphor that so many couples described. Thinking of marriage as a team sport gives us a way to name the unnamable. It gives us words to describe something that's often invisible, that easily gets lost in the battle for fairness: the third entity in marriage.

We realize that sounds strange. But here's what we mean. If you think about your arguments and conflicts with your partner, they generally involve two things: you and your partner. The fight over time spent with in-laws, where to go for a summer vacation, or whether you need a new lawn mower—that's a conflict of what's best for me versus what's best for you. When we think of marriage as a team sport, however, we begin to see that there's a third entity, another factor that has to be considered. It's your shared success. It's your team.

This insight changed everything for us. For the first decade or so of being together, our life was structured around the 50/50 habit of viewing our individual projects, careers, and goals as separate. Sure, we celebrated each other's wins. But we also lived with a subtle sense that we each had to protect our turf from the encroachments of the other person's work. In our conversations, there were only two interests at play: mine and yours.

Until one day, we realized the insanity of it all. On a date hike one spring morning (more on that later), we realized that we kept adding new projects, books, and events because it seemed good for one of us individually. The only problem was that it wasn't good for us as a couple or family. In fact, it was making us miserable. We both felt like we were racing through life, exhausted and overwhelmed.

And that's when it happened. We decided to run our own version of an 80/80 shared-success experiment. "What if we stopped viewing our professional lives as separate?" we asked. "What if we saw ourselves as part of something bigger, as a team? What if we structured all of life—our careers, parenting, logistics, and work around the house—around the question 'What's best for us?'"

It's an experiment that led us to restructure everything. But most important, it led us to name this new, third entity in our marriage. We called it Kajona (the combination of the first two letters of our two names and our daughter's).

Yes, we named our family the way you might name your breakout group at a motivational seminar or a corporate off-site. We understand how cheesy that might sound. But this new name gave us the vocabulary to change the conversation of marriage. Instead of defaulting to the worst of our 50/50 habits—asking, "What's best for me?"—we could now address the challenges in life by asking, "What's best for us?" Or in our case, "What's best for Kajona?" In short, this new name allowed us to remember and prioritize the essential third entity in marriage: our team.

The Benefits of Shared Success

There's a tiny voice inside all of us that might resist this idea. It's that part of us that has spent a lifetime hearing phrases like "Be all you can be," "Achieve your potential," and "Dream bigger," soaking in our culture's obsession with individual excellence. We all have this part of us, and we all might feel some anxiety about losing it, about giving up our own purpose, ambitions, and success to be with our partner.

It's an understandable fear. But it's also one that is easy to dispel. The 80/80 model isn't about giving up your individual identity in the name of shared success. In fact, this is yet another reason why we've called it the 80/80 model, not the 100/100 model. This isn't a 100 percent shift toward shared success that involves abandoning all of our individual projects, hopes, dreams, and preferences. There's still room for you in this model. The big shift in this 80/80 model is that we're now prioritizing the two of us together—our shared success—over our separate wins as individuals.

And yet this tiny voice might still be wondering: Why should I push myself toward this edge of shared success? Why should I step outside the familiar ground of doing what's best for me?

Consider a few of the most powerful benefits that arise from this shift:

Moving from Confusion to Clarity

The shift to a structure of shared success streamlines the chaos of married life. And that's no small thing. By getting clearer on your roles, priorities, and boundaries, you move from the rigid gender roles of the 80/20 model or the utter confusion of the 50/50 model to a clearer, more dynamic structure that supports the complicated logistics of modern family life.

Getting More Done, More Creatively, Together

When you see your lives as part of a joint project, you both end up with exponentially more creative and productive energy to handle life's challenges. And yet it's not just that you get more done. You also get the *right* things done. In a world where we are continually distracted and deluged by emails, texts, and messages, moving together in the same direction out of a shared set of values allows you to focus on the things that matter, rather than reactively saying yes to everything that matters to others.

Deeper Connection

It's great to have more clarity. It's amazing to become more creative and productive as a couple. But when it comes down to it, the real goal of the 80/80 model isn't getting organized or getting more stuff done. The real goal is to streamline the logistics of life so you can focus on what really matters: feeling more connected and in sync with your partner. In fact, it's fair to say that the strength of the whole enterprise of marriage is built on connection. When you have it, things are amazing. You're efficient. You joke around with each other. You laugh. You stay up late talking in bed. You have morning sex before work. When you don't, everything gets serious. You're too tense to laugh. You're spending so much time and energy bickering with each other that it's impossible to relax or get anything done. In short, without connection, sharing a life together quickly turns into a grueling, lifelong grind through conflict, misunderstanding, and resentment.

Winning at the Game of Marriage and Life

If marriage is a team sport, then the next question becomes: What's the game you and your partner want to win? This is an essential question. In speaking with numerous couples, we were struck by the fact that there is no single definition of shared success. Each couple, we found, has its own, idiosyncratic way of deciding what counts as a win together.

For some couples, success means achieving financial security. For others, it means the ability to travel the world and experience different cultures. For others, it means building a community of close friends and neighbors. For others, it means having a positive impact on the world. For others, it means having outrageously good sex. And for many couples, success arises from some combination of these and other projects.

There is, in other words, no single model of shared success. It all depends on your values as a couple, on whether you value money, travel, community, impact, sex, or something else.

So the first step in building this new structure of shared success is to begin figuring out what shared success means for you and your partner—in other words, to identify your shared values of success.

Your Shared Values of Success

The goal of this exercise is to choose between one and five core values that define shared success for you and your partner. To do this, we invite you and your partner to complete a brief exercise, separately at first and then together.

Step 1: Circle your top three to five guiding values for your team. (If you notice some of your key values are missing, add them in the blank spaces below.)

Adventure	Wealth creation	Volunteering
Travel	Physical fitness	Political activism
Family time	Mental fitness	Time in nature
Impact	Spiritual growth	Feeling at home
Philanthropy	Amazing sex	Fun
Professional achievements	Creativity	Pushing your edge
Building community	Mentoring	Excitement
Cultivating friendships	Sustainability	Planning for retirement

Step 2: List each of your top five values of shared success

PARTNER 1	PARTNER 2
Value 1:	Value 1:
Value 2:	Value 2:
Value 3:	Value 3:
Value 4:	Value 4:
Value 5:	Value 5:

Step 3: Come up with a combined list of your values of shared success

Now that you both have your lists, take some time to talk about them. Use your individual lists as the starting point for coming up with a list of the three to five values that make up your shared values of success. Then write them out in order of priority below.

YOUR VALUES OF SHARED SUCCESS

Value 1: _____

Value 2: _____

Value 3: _____

Value 4: _____

Value 5: _____

Tip 1: What do you do if you don't have any shared values?

Two options. First, try consolidating both lists into one larger list. Then, together as a team, see if you can identify the top three to five values. Second, try coming up with a shared list of three to five values again, together as a team.

Tip 2: What's that spirit we keep talking about?

Radical generosity. We know that we've left the mindset section of the book, but a conversation like this is the perfect time to see if you can stay connected to this spirit of radical generosity.

Tip 3: Create a visual reminder of your shared values

If you are like most people, you will quickly forget all about these values. So we recommend putting them up somewhere impossible to miss: the kitchen counter, your bathroom mirror, or the doorway in from the garage. We keep ours on a small chalkboard in the kitchen.

Want a More Advanced Practice?

Remember how we named our team Kajona? Now it's time for you to do the same with the advanced practice:

GIVE YOUR FAMILY TEAM A NAME

It could be called Team Smith, Epic, the Three Amigos, or whatever other wild idea you come up with.

Tip 1: Build the habit of using this name

Once you land on a name together, make a habit of using this name whenever the conversation turns to your shared work together.

Tip 2: RG

Radical generosity, always.

Identifying these values is the first step in structuring your marriage around shared success. The next step is to use them to design a structure of life for navigating the five elements that throw off even the most stable relationships: roles, priorities, boundaries, power, and sex.

CHAPTER 9

Roles—Who Does What?

Here's a conversation that we had approximately ten thousand times in the early years of our marriage.

> *Kaley:* It looks like a bomb went off in our grill outside. Can you take the lead on cleaning it?
>
> *Nate:* I'm on it. I just put it on my list.

One week later . . .

> *Kaley:* I notice nothing happened with the grill. When are you going to get that clean?
>
> *Nate:* It's on my list, babe. I'm telling you. I got it.

Three weeks later . . .

> *Kaley:* I can't figure out what the hell is going on with this "list" of yours. The grill still looks horrible. Are you going to clean it? Or do I need to do it myself?
>
> *Nate:* You realize that the more you nag me, the less I want to ever clean the stupid grill.

Somewhere around the ten thousand and fifth time this happened, we realized what was going on here. It's a dynamic that we now know isn't unique to us; this strange phenomenon has been reported by many couples. It's a pattern in which delegation leads to resentment, and resentment leads to an all-out marital explosion.

Welcome to the Delegate-Resent-Explode Cycle

In most relationships, one partner is first to see the ketchup stains on the shelf of the refrigerator door. One partner is first to notice that if you don't renew the registration for your car, it won't be street legal next month. One partner is first to notice that it's your turn to host dinner with friends.

While one partner is sitting on the couch binge-watching *Game of Thrones*, this more responsible partner can't help but notice the daily procession of problems, cracks, breaks, and logistics. This leaves the partner who cares more about the logistics of domestic life with two choices. Choice one: they can do literally everything themselves, a recipe for a lifetime of bitterness and resentment toward their mate. Or choice two: they can step into the role of domestic drill sergeant, barking out orders to their partner. "Unload the dishwasher, please." "Dustbuster under Junior's car seat, please." "Take Rover out for a walk, please, and while you're at it, can you pick up his poop off the front lawn with this grocery bag?"

It's a tough choice: live in resentment or delegate to your partner like he or she is some sort of clueless college summer intern. For most people, the second option seems like the best path.

But as we learned ourselves, this second path of delegation is the perfect recipe for resentment.

Delegation is designed for the office. It's what managers do to their direct reports, what CEOs do to their EAs, what factory foremen do to their workers. And it works at the office because everyone has a clear understanding of their role in the organization.

But marriage and relationships are different. When you have a husband, a wife, or a serious boyfriend or girlfriend, the dynamic of delegation falls apart. You are supposed to be equals, after all. That's the whole innovation of the 50/50 model. So why should one of you wield power over the other like a domestic autocrat? Why should one of you be the family taskmaster and the other the marital underling?

It's questions like these that show why delegation turns to resentment. One partner becomes the de facto boss in one or more areas and the other starts to resent them for it. In our case, each time Kaley asked, "When are you going to clean the damn grill?" Nate felt like he was back at his summer job as a twenty-year-old, standing in the back room of the local Domino's Pizza franchise, receiving orders from his store manager about how best to break down grease-stained pizza boxes at the end of a shift. And so, just as Nate had resented his perpetually stoned pizza store manager, he started to resent Kaley.

And when resentment builds, it can quickly turn to an all-out explosion of rage or passive-aggressiveness. That's the real reason why Nate never cleaned the grill. His resentment-fueled explosion took the form of a passive-aggressive domestic labor strike. Sure, he could have just followed orders like a yes-man and cleaned the grill. But he had reached his resentment threshold. And so he resorted to one of the oldest, least mature tricks in the marital book: saying he would do something, knowing that he wouldn't, and then doing nothing.

This passive act of resistance infuriated Kaley, who then launched into a verbal tirade about Nate not pulling his weight, not following through, and not caring enough. And that's how these conflicts usually end: with an explosion of tears, hurt feelings, and lingering rage.

As you probably know from your own experience, getting caught in this cycle sucks. It's a recipe for conflict. It's also about as efficient as spending your workdays scanning Instagram or battling with your friends in a seven-hour game of *Fortnite*. And the most tragic aspect of this delegate-resent-explode cycle is that it prevents us from getting what we really want out of marriage: love, intimacy, and deep connection.

The Reason We Get Stuck

There's a relatively simple explanation for why we get caught in this cycle: role confusion. Our 80/20 ancestors didn't really have this problem. They may have lived with crippling inequality and blatant sexism, but most couples had no problem coming up with a structure of roles. That's not because they were smarter or more conscious than we are. It's because the cultural norms of the time did all the heavy lifting for them. Men did "men stuff": finances, work at the office, binge-drinking, and lawn mowing. Women did "women stuff": cooking, cleaning, gossiping, binge-smoking, and taking care of the kids.

With the rise of gender equality and the 50/50 model, however, clarity turned to confusion. The roles and responsibilities of each partner were now assumed to be equal and fair. But what does that mean? Does it mean everybody does everything? Does it mean we divide up the tasks randomly? Or does it mean we just wing it and see what happens when we let old habits and historical accident shape our roles and responsibilities?

If you're like most couples, you have probably taken a wing-it approach to roles. We saw this again and again in our conversations with couples. When we asked how they determined roles and responsibilities, most people would pause for an awkwardly long time. They would then hesitantly answer, "Well, I guess we never really thought about roles. It just kind of happened." As one man observed, "I'm the toothbrush guy with our daughter. I have no idea why that happened. But ninety percent of the time, I'm the guy."

The wing-it approach to roles is a hallmark of the 50/50 model. For some couples, it works. But for most, it leads to confusion, chaos, and conflict. As one woman we interviewed observed, "This cycle happens every six to eight weeks, religiously. There will be an event that breaks the camel's back, where I get to a point where I feel like I'm coming un-done, and I'm stressed and it's not fair and there is too much on my plate. There will be tears. He will get defensive. We will finally talk it out and it gets better for a short time. Then six to eight weeks later, it happens again."

Role confusion is what keeps this problem coming back. It's a bad marital habit that leads to three big problems.

Problem 1: Inequality

It's no accident that in even the most progressive households, even when a woman out earns her male partner, women often find themselves doing the bulk of the work around the house. That's the lingering traces of the 80/20 model slipping into modern marriage. And those traces lead to inequality, structures in which one person in the relationship (generally the woman) takes on a disproportionate share of the domestic labor.

Problem 2: Inefficiency

When roles are clear, each small task or to-do gets done by the part-ner who owns that domain. Completion is quick and almost automatic. When roles become confused, each small task or to-do becomes like a city council meeting—a jumping-off point for discussion instead of ac-tion. That's why role confusion is so maddeningly inefficient: instead of just dragging the garbage cans out to the curb, we're lost in the time-sucking discussion of why we should do it, who should do it, and when it needs to get done.

Problem 3:
Volatility, Uncertainty, Complexity, and Ambiguity

Role confusion leads to what military strategists call VUCA—a state of volatility, uncertainty, complexity, and ambiguity. "Did the credit card get paid?" "Who knows?" "Did somebody pick up our kid from camp?" "Who knows?" Role confusion creates a structure in which nobody ever really knows whether anything got done. Living a VUCA life in your marriage is like wandering around in a pitch-black room. You never quite know when you're going to slam into a wall or stub your toe on an invisible stair or impale yourself on a shower rod.

And that's why in the end, this wing-it approach to roles in marriage creates chaos, confusion, and all sorts of unnecessary drama. The failure of role confusion sets up one of the central insights of shared success in the 80/80 model: the idea that structure matters. By spending a short amount of time establishing clear roles, you create clarity, efficiency, and greater ease throughout the system.

Roles Built for Shared Success

You may resist this idea of thinking about roles and responsibilities. You may think talk of clear roles is about as sexy as a multi-tabbed Excel spreadsheet or an explanation of exchange-traded forwards on the Nasdaq derivatives market. But like it or not, every couple already has a structure of roles and responsibilities. It's a structure that's either clear and created consciously, or confused and unconscious, buried beneath the surface of married life, ready to explode at any moment.

To see the power of a finely tuned structure of roles, consider Andrew and Jon, a couple who recently adopted a baby boy—a life-altering transition that forced them to rethink their roles and responsibilities.

As consultants in their day jobs, Andrew and Jon decided to come up with an alternative to the wing-it approach. They understood the value of efficiency and the cost savings that come with clear systems. So they thought hard about a better way of deciding who does what. Jon told us, "The most important thing is to play to each other's strengths. I do all the bills and finances because they take less emotional labor and burden for me. It doesn't cause me anxiety. For Andrew, on the other hand, it's a huge burden." The goal of dividing tasks, in other words, is largely about efficiency. As Jon put it, "We try to think, What can we do well with the least amount of energy?"

And yet efficiency isn't the only thing driving this structure of shared success. They also consider interest in the task. Early on, for instance, they realized that Andrew had a greater level of interest in spending long stretches of time with their child. This, coupled with Jon's acumen for financial tasks, led them to set up a structure in which Jon takes the lead on managing the house and Andrew takes the lead on managing childcare.

Andrew and Jon also built their roles around a concept that they call "service level." They define service level as the expectations each person has for a given task. As Andrew explains, "In any couple, you have a different service level for your expectations for how clean the floor needs to be. I'm willing to walk around in bare feet on a sticky gross floor; Jon isn't." If one person has to have a spotless kitchen, in other words, their service level for that task is high. If the other doesn't care, their service level is low. This insight led them to a powerful realization: if one person has a higher service level, it makes the most sense for him to either own the task or be in charge of outsourcing it. The high-service-level partner, after all, will see problems that need to be addressed long before the low-service-level partner.

Andrew and Jon's strategy for dividing roles points to a promising alternative to the wing-it strategy. Their structure minimizes tension and conflict. It creates clarity instead of confusion. Most important, it's a structure built around the idea that the two of them are a team, working together to achieve shared success.

This intentional approach represents the intersection of shared success and the messy task of dividing up all the to-dos, tasks, and chores of sharing a life together. Instead of letting history and habits lead us into the inequality of the 80/20 model or the confusion of the 50/50 model, we can build a dynamic structure of roles customized to fit our unique values, strengths, and interests. It's an exercise that enables us to build the core values of 80/80 deep into the fabric of everyday life. By streamlining our roles, we shift from a life of confusion, drama, and fairness fights to one based on radical generosity and shared success.

Five Role Guidelines for Shared Success

When it comes to the question of how best to build this new structure, consider these five primary guidelines:

Guideline 1: Skill

Let's face it, some people are just better at hanging a picture on the wall. Some are better at childcare. Some are better at climbing up a ladder and nailing Christmas lights to the roof of the garage. Skill matters when it comes to structuring your roles. So as you think through your division of labor, consider: Is one of you significantly better and more efficient at certain tasks than the other?

Guideline 2: Interest

Just as you each have unique skills, you also have distinct desires and interests. Some people find washing dishes intolerable. Others find that scrubbing crumbs off the plate is a pathway to meditative bliss. Some people love yard work. Others have an allergy attack the moment the first blade of grass gets cut. So it's worth asking: Does one of you have significantly more or less interest in certain tasks?

Guideline 3: Standards

It's important to account for each partner's expectations for what counts as satisfactory. Andrew and Jon called this service level. We call these standards. Your standards define the point at which a dirty toilet, a sidewalk with unshoveled snow, or a disorganized vacation itinerary becomes a problem. In each relationship, partners have higher or lower standards for various tasks. If you can't stand the sight of a single dandelion popping up on the grass in spring and your partner doesn't care, you have higher standards for landscaping. If your partner spends hours each month creating elaborate financial reports on family spending that you find unnecessary, your partner has higher standards for finance. Once you identify these differences, you can begin to take into account the central insight of standards: the fact that, all things being equal, the partner with higher standards for a particular task will do a better job completing the task or outsourcing it to someone else.

Guideline 4: Shared Success

By now, you're familiar with the primary structural insight of the 80/80 marriage: structure your life not around fairness or your competing individual aims, but around your values of shared success. Nowhere are these shared values more important than in creating your roles. The ordinary 50/50 approach to roles, after all, is to try to make everything fair—to find the perfect 50/50 midpoint of task distribution. In the 80/80 approach, by contrast, we let what's best for *us*—our shared values— determine the structure of our roles. This means it's not always about equal division or fairness. Consider the couple with a high-earning partner who loves her work and a lower-earning partner who wants to scale his time back to take on more of the childcare. Their division of household roles might not be "fair" in the 50/50 sense. The husband might take on more of the domestic work, while the wife takes on more of the earning potential. This arrangement might work well for them because it aligns with their values of shared success. Of course, some couples might have a different shared vision. They might decide to both go all out in their careers and divide up domestic roles evenly. This approach might work best for them. The point is to let shared success—not 50/50 fairness—determine your structure of roles.

Guideline 5: Outsourcing

There are some tasks in marriage that neither person is particularly good at and neither person wants to do. There are also times when one person's standards are higher across the board, and no matter how hard the other partner tries, he or she can never meet expectations. In these cases, if you have the financial resources to do so, outsourcing can be an excellent option. If you can't get aligned on bathroom cleanliness, hire a housecleaner. If neither of you wants to weed the backyard, hire a gardener. It's also worth noting that outsourcing doesn't always cost money. When it comes to childcare, for instance, grandparents and other family members are often happy to provide outside support.

For many couples, creating a new structure of roles based on these five guidelines is essential to building a structure of shared success. This was certainly true for us. In fact, we both remember the day it happened. It was just a few weeks after the daycare-pickup-time fight that almost ended our marriage. We sat down at the kitchen table with two blank sheets of paper. On the first sheet, we wrote out one column with Kaley's current roles and one column with Nate's current roles. Once we had everything down on paper, the source of our tension became clear. We could see that Kaley needed support. We could see why she had to delegate so much—she was taking on a disproportionate share of the responsibilities, an arrangement that didn't align with our values of shared success. We could also see that our roles weren't aligned with our skills or interests.

We then took the next few minutes to write out a new, more efficient, and more fulfilling distribution of our roles on the second sheet. In all, the entire exercise took about twenty minutes. And yet it ended the toxic struggle we had been engaged in. It's been seven years since that moment. We've certainly argued and disagreed about things since then. But we now each own our lanes. We get stuff done. When conflicts arise, we see this as feedback that something is off with our roles. So instead of torturing each other with passive-aggressive labor strikes or patronizing comments, we simply adjust the structure of our roles to bring things back into balance.

Now it's your turn to come up with your own alternative. It's time to create a new, more efficient and meaningful structure of roles built to ensure that when it comes to who does what, you both win together.

Roles for Shared Success

80/80 PRACTICE

To streamline your life for shared success, take some time to define your structure of roles.

Step 1: Write out your current roles

These roles fall into three primary categories: Partner 1's, Partner 2's, and Shared (the roles neither partner owns). Here are some examples of the tasks that most often show up in marriage. Note when you own a particular task, that becomes your role.

Cleaning	Scheduling playdates	Buying groceries
Doing laundry	Managing the social calendar	Basic finances
Fixing things	Hosting friends	Paying taxes
Doing yardwork	Cooking	Overseeing investments
Vacation planning	Doing dishes	Caring for sick kids
Planning kids' camps	Taking out the trash	Caring for aging parents
Planning events	Servicing car(s)	Managing school logistics

PARTNER 1 (Tasks you manage alone)	SHARED (Tasks you manage together)	PARTNER 2 (Tasks you manage alone)
1.	1.	1.
2.	2.	2.
3.	3.	3.
3.	3.	3.
4.	4.	4.
5.	5.	5.
6.	6.	6.
7.	7.	7.
8.	8.	8.
9.	9.	9.
10.	10.	10.
11.	11.	11.
12.	12.	12.

13.	13.	13.
14.	14.	14.
15.	15.	15.
16.	16.	16.

Step 2: Evaluate your current structure of roles

Take a moment to reflect on what's working and what's not. Remember to consider the five role guidelines for shared success:

- Skill: Are you in roles that match your skills?
- Interest: Do you enjoy carrying out the roles that you are in?
- Standards: Do you have radically different standards for some of these tasks?
- Shared Success: Does your current distribution of roles reflect your values of shared success? How can you make this structure line up with the spirit of "What's best for us?"
- Outsourcing: Do you have the resources to outsource roles neither of you wants to own?

Tip 1: Limit your shared roles

While most couples maintain some shared roles after this exercise (things like cooking, doing dishes, or picking up the kids from school), make sure this category doesn't grow too large. We recommend sharing no more than 25 percent of your roles. The more roles you share, the more room there is for conflict.

Tip 2: Radical generosity

To make this all work, remember—keep it radically generous.

Step 3: Create your new structure of roles

The final step is to work together to come up with a new, more intentional, structure of roles.

PARTNER 1 (Tasks you manage alone)	SHARED (Tasks you manage together)	PARTNER 2 (Tasks you manage alone)
1.	1.	1.
2.	2.	2.
3.	3.	3.
4.	4.	4.
5.	5.	5.
6.	6.	6.
7.	7.	7.
8.	8.	8.
9.	9.	9.
10.	10.	10.
11.	11.	11.
12.	12.	12.
13.	13.	13.
14.	14.	14.
15.	15.	15.
16.	16.	16.

Now that you have a clearer understanding of roles, the next step in building an 80/80 structure is to explore what to say yes to in life (your priorities) and what to say no to (your boundaries).

CHAPTER 10

Priorities—What's Your Yes?

Carrie Dorr seems like a woman who has it all.

She grew up in Detroit thinking she wanted to become a lawyer. But her true love was always fitness and dance. So even after she landed her first job at a big corporate law firm, she continued to teach dance at night as a side hustle. Then one day, she left her law career behind. She opened a studio.

People loved her classes and soon her single dance studio turned into two and then ten and then five hundred. Her big idea that you could bring together fitness and dance came to be known as Pure Barre—one of the most influential boutique fitness brands in the world.

Carrie spent eleven years building this business. It was difficult, time-consuming, and at times overwhelming. But it wasn't nearly as difficult as her next big venture: raising three children, all born fewer than three years apart, with her husband, Frank.

As Carrie describes the challenge of this new situation: "You get one cup in life. You don't get separate cups of energy, one for your marriage, one for your kids, one for your work. It's just one big cup and everyone sips out of it every single day."

Having one cup isn't new. Husbands and wives in the 1950s also had only one cup in life. The difference is that they didn't have as many things draining it. They didn't have the "always on," 24-7 workday. They didn't have breaking-news updates or twenty-four-hour cable news networks. They didn't receive a continual stream of texts, notifications, and emails from friends, family members, and random people trying to sell them stuff they didn't need. And they definitely didn't feel the irresistible urge to pull out their phone at all hours of the day—all so they could surf Instagram to see how much more fun their friends were having in life.

This overload, the chaos of modern life, explains why so many people, like Carrie, find it difficult to balance and prioritize all of life's demands. When you add kids to the already overwhelming context of modern life, it can begin to feel like there's never enough time and energy. As she explains, "The biggest challenge with kids is finding enough mental time for your spouse. All the operational stuff that needs to be done to run the household sucks all the energy out of the cup. Before kids, I had enough mental space to put a lot of thought into my marriage. I would ask my husband questions about his dad or his brother. Now there's just too much information to possibly manage it all. It feels like a total computer meltdown sometimes."

Carrie wasn't the only one to tell us about this modern predicament. This complaint was perhaps the most frequently voiced concern shared by the couples we interviewed. "There's no time," they told us. "There's too much to do." "We're stretched thin." "We can't ever seem to fit it all in."

The You-Can-Have-It-All Culture

We've always lived in a culture that celebrates success. And yet over the past few decades, we seem to be striving for something more like success on steroids. It's a strange new aspiration, best summed up by the belief that you can "have it all."

This wasn't always the case. It used to be enough to do one thing well. You could be a brilliant writer or an amazing athlete or an inspirational teacher or a successful businessperson or a devoted stay-at-home parent—you didn't have to be all five. With the rise of the 50/50 model, however, it's no longer enough to be great at just one thing. We've set a new cultural goal—to be great at, well, everything.

This perverse new goal weighs most heavily on women. As Gloria Steinem explains, "You can work full time in the paid labor force, only if you keep on working full time in the unpaid labor force. You cook three gourmet meals a day, you raise two perfect children, you dress for success, and as a women's magazine once put it, you are 'multi-orgasmic till dawn.'"[1] This leaves professional women feeling the guilt of not being home more, and it leaves stay-at-home moms with the nagging feeling that they should be doing more to advance professionally. It leaves most women feeling that to truly succeed, you have to become a modern-day superwoman—effortlessly amazing in all areas of life.

And yet this new cultural ideal also weighs heavily on men. During the early stages of the 2020 coronavirus pandemic, for example, one influencer on Twitter remarked:

If you don't come out of this quarantine with:

A new skill you learned
Starting your side hustle
More knowledge

You never lacked time. You lacked discipline.[2]

Starting your side hustle, sculpting your six-pack, and reading the complete works of Aristotle, all during a global pandemic and economic meltdown—why not? You can have it all.

The real problem with this message is that it makes setting priorities impossible. In the days of 80/20, one partner, generally the man, prioritized work. The other, generally the woman, prioritized parenting and managing the house. Husbands didn't beat themselves up for not being fully present at home. Wives didn't get mom-shamed for missing a Little League game to attend a work meeting, because there were no work meetings to attend. Priorities back then were simple.

Now, however, to have it all, you have to prioritize it all. Howard H. Stevenson, the chair of Harvard Business Publishing, offers the perfect analogy for this approach. It's like "walking on a balance beam while trying to juggle an egg, a crystal glass, a knife, and any number of other fragile or hazardous objects."[3] Put simply, it's impossible.

The Hidden Virtue of Failing in Life

By now, two things should be clear. First, there's no such thing as having it all in married life, especially with kids. Second, we need a better approach to priorities. If we prioritize everything, then we end up effectively prioritizing nothing.

Consider Susan. You might remember her from the introduction. She's the one who told us, "I'm used to getting an A-plus in life, but I'm spread so thin right now that everyone in my life—my husband, my kids, my employees—gets a C or a C-minus from me."

After talking with Susan, we were struck by her statement that everyone gets a C from her. The more we reflected on it, the more we began to see her impromptu life report card less as an admission of failure and more as an act of wise acceptance, a letting-go of the idea that she should get all A's in life.

Susan helped us see that unlike in school, where if you were one of those overachiever types, getting all A's was possible, there is no such thing as a life valedictorian. Life is more like going to a school where you're enrolled in a hundred different classes that meet constantly and at all hours of the day and night. To succeed across all subjects, just think about everything you would have to master: the required course in Being a Badass at Work, Being an Amazing Lover 101, the survey course in Mastering the Modern Art of Hyper-Parenting, the senior seminar in Working Out Daily, the 200-level class in Caring for Your Aging Parents, and so on.

And yet the bigger problem is: in life, getting an A in just one or two of these courses effectively destroys your ability to get an A in many of the others. If you decide to become a corporate superstar and get an A-plus in your career, you now say yes to every business trip, you work nights and weekends, and you play the politics of face time at the office, which means there is no way you can make it to all your kids' T-ball games, school events, and piano recitals. Your A-plus in your career destroys your ability to get an A at home. Conversely, if you decide to get an A-plus in parenting by joining the PTO, making banana bread from scratch for the school bake sale, shuttling your children to games and recitals, planning playdates, and being the room parent at school, your A-plus in parenting destroys your ability to get an A in your career.

All of this leads us to the hard truth of modern life. We can't get all A's in life. And without clear priorities, we're unlikely to get any A's at all. In fact, without priorities, we seem to naturally slip into the trap set by our you-can-have-it-all culture of trying to do everything well, feeling shame, inner criticism, and embarrassment when we don't, and then giving up altogether on having priorities and just responding randomly to the incoming demands of life.

We think there's a better way to respond to this hard truth. What if we redefined success as getting only a couple of A's in life? What if bringing our full focus and attention to one or two things was the ultimate life achievement? And what if we were willing, even excited, to fail at the rest of life?

The basic approach here is to pick a few areas to prioritize and then willingly accept getting C's, D's, and F's in many of the other subjects of life. This sounds like a strange aspiration, but it's actually liberating. To know that the best you can give at work right now is a B allows you to loosen your grip on perfectionism. To know that you're shooting for a D-minus in parental involvement at your kid's school allows you to send store-bought cookies to your son's end-of-year class party with no shame. In fact, you're now an overachiever because D-minus parents probably don't even send cookies at all. It sounds crazy. But accepting your C's, D's, and F's in life frees up more energy to direct toward the handful of subjects that matter most to you.

Of course, you might be thinking to yourself, "I'm too busy to sit around sorting out my priorities." But without clear priorities, you're letting your peripheral friends, colleagues at work, extended family members, and requests from random people you have never even met rule your life. As Greg McKeown, author of *Essentialism*, declares, "If you don't prioritize your life, someone else will."[4] With clear priorities, on the other hand, you are putting yourself in control. You are giving yourself the courage and clarity to fail in some life classes that don't matter and get an A or two in the ones that matter most to you.

How do you identify these priorities and line them up with your partner's? That's the goal of the Life Report Card. It's your chance to decide where you want to excel in life and where you are willing to just barely pass or even fail.

The Life Report Card

80/80 PRACTICE

The goal of this practice is to give you a chance to candidly assess your grades in subjects that span the full spectrum of activities in life and in marriage. You will first fill out your *actual grades*, which reflect your current level of effort in each of these areas. Be brutally honest here. You will then fill out your *ideal grades*, those that reflect your highest priorities. Be realistic here. Most important, as you fill out your ideal grades, make sure your priorities reflect your shared values of success as a couple.

Tip 1: Give up on perfection

Remember, don't try to "have it all" by being a life valedictorian. It's hopeless. Limit yourself to one to three A's.

Tip 2: Look forward to failure

As you consider your ideal grades, don't be afraid to fail. C's, D's, and F's are a good thing in this practice. By failing in some subjects, you free up more energy to do well in the one or two that matter most to you.

Tip 3: Customize your subject list

Don't see some of your most important life subjects? Add those in the blank lines at the bottom.

Step 1: Fill out your individual Life Report Cards

PARTNER 1

SUBJECTS	ACTUAL GRADE SCALE	IDEAL GRADE SCALE	COMMENTS
	A: Excellent B: Good C: Satisfactory D: Poor F: Failure N/A: Not applicable	A: Excellent B: Good C: Satisfactory D: Poor F: Failure N/A: Not applicable	*If the ideal grade is different from the actual grade, what needs to change to prioritize or deprioritize this subject?*
Housework			
Parenting			
Career			
Personal growth			
Friends/ family time			
Couple time			
Community involvement			

Spirituality			
Travel			
Exercise			
Political activism			
Learning			
Rest time			
Life logistics			
Total number of A's (No more than 1–3)			

PARTNER 2

SUBJECTS	ACTUAL GRADE SCALE	IDEAL GRADE SCALE	COMMENTS
	A: Excellent B: Good C: Satisfactory D: Poor F: Failure N/A: Not applicable	A: Excellent B: Good C: Satisfactory D: Poor F: Failure N/A: Not applicable	*If the ideal grade is different from the actual grade, what needs to change to prioritize or deprioritize this subject?*
Housework			
Parenting			
Career			
Personal growth			

Friends/ family time			
Couple time			
Community involvement			
Spirituality			
Travel			
Exercise			
Political activism			
Learning			
Rest time			
Life logistics			
Total number of A's (No more than 1–3)			

Step 2: Share your report card with your partner and make sure your priorities lead to shared success

Talk with your partner about the priorities expressed through your actual and ideal grades. Your report cards reflect your individual priorities, but ideally, the combination of your two report cards should reflect your values of shared success as well. To make this happen, first go back to your shared values of success as a reminder of what it looks like for the two of you to win together. Then consider the following questions:

Does directing more energy to my A's help us win together?
Does putting less energy into my C's, D's, and F's help us win
together?

What do you do if your values of shared success don't line up with
your priorities, or if you think your partner has the wrong priorities? That's the perfect time to talk together about any adjustments
you need to make to your individual report cards. Remember, it's
perfectly fine to have different priorities. The goal of this exercise
isn't to arrive at the same individual lists of priorities. Instead, the
goal is to connect these lists to the larger aim of shared success.

Tip: Stay in the 80/80 mindset

If disagreements come up or if you feel irritated, remember to
Reveal and Request, and stay in the spirit of radical generosity,
always.

CHAPTER 11

Boundaries—What's Your No?

Once upon a time, in a suburban land filled with Starbucks coffee-houses and P.F. Chang's franchises, there lived a husband and wife. On paper, they seemed to have it all: two kids, a nice home, and enough money in the bank to rest easy at night. They were the kind of couple who sends out those glorious Christmas cards during the holidays, in which everyone in the family looks so happy and adorable, you start to wonder whether they missed their true calling in catalog modeling.

This couple professed clear priorities of shared success: get a B-plus in work, an A in parenting, an A in spending time together as a couple, and C's, D's, and F's in the rest of life's subjects. They just had one problem, a small imperfection, that made their lives miserable. They couldn't seem to say the word *no*.

When the husband's manager texted a series of random questions during family time, he walked away from the game of Uno for ten minutes to respond because that's what good employees do. When the wife picked up her cell phone at a Little League game and saw an incoming call from a coworker, she answered and spent the next twenty minutes talking about office drama because that's what good coworkers do.

When both sets of parents called to ask about visiting this year for an extra week, the couple said yes because hosting parents for long stretches is what good adult children do. When the two of them went to the beach for their once-a-year date-vacation and found out a good friend was staying nearby, they skipped having dinner together and met up for drinks and dinner with their friend because that's what good friends do.

And yet in those rare moments when they finally did have time alone, the same conversation came up again and again. "We say parenting and time alone together are our top priorities, so why do we keep getting a C in parenting and an F in spending time alone together? Why are we constantly overwhelmed by life and unable to do what we really want?"

They're not alone. In fact, this couple is the two of us. This couple is you and your partner. On some level, this couple is all of us.

The Problem with Never Saying No

From the outside, the problem is obvious: it's not enough to have clear priorities. It's not enough to know what to say yes to in marriage and in life. We also need boundaries, clear nos to the daily onslaught of tasks, projects, and offers that threaten to keep us distracted from what matters most: our values of shared success. In short, we can't just say yes to the things that matter. We also have to say no to the things that don't.

The problem is that saying yes is easy. Saying no, on the other hand, often isn't. When your boss tells you, "I know you're on your anniversary trip in Cancún next week, but can't you just throw on a dress shirt over your swimsuit and jump on the Zoom call for a half hour?" it's easier to say yes than no. When your relatives tell you, "We would love to crash at your house over Labor Day weekend," it's easier to say yes than no. When your neighbor says, "I know you put in the fence between our houses a few years ago, but I want to upgrade it this year to premium redwood, and I'm hoping you'll cover half the cost," it's easier to say yes than no.

If you look carefully at these asks from others, you start to see that they come in three primary forms.

1. The Invitation

"Are you two interested in coming by for dinner on Saturday?" "Would you like to fly to Orlando to give a presentation at our trade show?" "Are you willing to stop by our fundraiser on Thursday?" These are the sounds of the invitation—an earnest request for your time that seems like it's in everyone's best interest. Sometimes these invitations match your priorities. You meet them with an effortless yes that rolls right off the tongue. But sometimes they don't. Sometimes the dinner at a friend's house on Saturday interferes with date night that week. Sometimes the trip to Orlando forces you to miss your kid's school talent show. In these moments, saying yes and failing to set a clear boundary can come at a high cost: your priorities.

2. The Request

"I know you're busy, but could you spare thirty minutes to meet for coffee next week?" "Could you give me some feedback on my PowerPoint deck?" "Can you come by and help us move some furniture out of the garage?" These are the sounds of the request—an ask for your time that may not be in your best interest but would be helpful to the other person. Here again, sometimes it makes sense to say yes. Sometimes these requests are easy to fulfill. They can also be a way to help and contribute to the lives of others. And yet, say yes to too many of these requests and soon there's no time left for what matters most to you and your partner.

3. The Demand

"You two haven't visited us for Christmas in three years. We need you here this year." "I can't make the meeting in Los Angeles next month. I need you to cover for me." "You signed up for the neighborhood HOA meetings, so we need you there on Wednesday night." These are the sounds of the demand—the most forceful call for your time and energy. There may be times when it makes sense to say yes to these sorts of demands for your time. But here again, the habit of never pushing back, failing to set clear boundaries, or hesitating to offer a clear no can make it impossible to live out the priorities you outlined in the previous chapter.

It might seem like it's easiest to say no to invitations and most difficult to say no to demands. But for most of us, saying no to any of these calls for our time and attention is equally difficult. The reason is that it's just easier, at least in the short run, to follow the agreeable path of yes than to set a boundary by saying no. When you say yes, people laugh at your jokes, smile at you, and tell all their friends about what a great person you are. You become the good friend, the amazing neighbor, and the team player at work.

When you say no, in contrast, the whole world turns upside down. You might feel the guilt of letting down your friend, your coworker, or your family member. The people receiving your no mirror back this discomfort. They get upset, they give you funny looks, and they may even gossip about you behind your back. And why shouldn't they? You have just told them that your plan for your own life is more important than their plan for your life. How dare you?

The Most Difficult No

When it comes to boundaries, there are easy nos and difficult nos. The easy ones come up with people who have no real influence over the structure of your marriage. These are friends you occasionally see, extended family members you rarely talk to, or colleagues you meet with every now and then. These people are so far removed from the internal dynamics of your marriage that they pose no real threat to the system; as a result, it's easy to set boundaries with them.

But then there are those people or projects that pose a bigger boundary-setting challenge: your difficult nos. Author and marriage therapist Stan Tatkin calls these *thirds*. Thirds can be parents, children, and relatives. They can be close friends or coworkers. They can even be events and activities. Put simply, a third is any outside party or activity that attempts to exert influence on your system of shared success.[1]

Thirds usually don't see themselves as intruding. They are generally close to one partner but not the other. So from the perspective of the third, the invitation to come to a family brunch or the idea of planning a trip together isn't an intrusion. It's just an attempt to connect and make plans with someone they care about.

Why should you be on the lookout for the influence of thirds? First, your closest thirds have the potential to disrupt the delicate balance of power between you and your partner. For instance, let's say you and your partner spent months finding the right school for your child. Then, just before you sign the paperwork, your mother-in-law (an intimate third in your system) tries to talk your partner out of the decision, saying it would be better for your child to attend the school just a few blocks from her house.

This is the perfect setup for an epic fight. Why? Because a third has just intruded into your system of shared success. It's like a game of basketball in which your two-person team is driving the ball to the basket and suddenly a fan (in this case, your mother-in-law) jumps the railing and runs out onto the court, sending the whole game into chaos.

The second reason you should be on the lookout for the influence of thirds is that if your boundaries are weak, thirds will roll all over them. Parents, kids, friends, and coworkers all have their own priorities. They want you to spend more of your scarce vacation time visiting *them*. They want you to cancel a date night to attend *their* dinner party. They want you to take time away from your partner on a couples vacation to call in to *their* important work meetings. This isn't because they're acting with ill will or intentionally trying to disrupt your life. They simply have a vested interest in arranging circumstances so you spend more time with them.

So without clear boundaries, these thirds end up getting exactly what they want, while you and your partner get exactly what you don't want: feelings of resentment and betrayal that stoke the flames of conflict.

All of this is to say that it's worth paying close attention to the people in your life who exert the most outside influence and make it most difficult for you and your partner to set boundaries. These people or projects are your thirds. And while you love them and know that they're doing the best they can, living out your priorities will often require that you say no to their attempts to sway your family system.

The Art of No

What's the best way to set these boundaries? How should you say no? When it comes to the easy nos, here are just a few of the tactics you might consider:

- **The Priorities No:** This is saying no and then briefly explaining why the request doesn't fit your priorities of shared success. It's efficient and honest, and sometimes your clear expression of priorities can even inspire the other person. It's saying, "We would love to come to the barbecue, but the two of us haven't gone on a date night in weeks and it's really important to us to spend this time together."
- **The Delay Tactic:** This is buying you and your partner time by saying, "I'm not sure what we're up to this weekend. We'll check our calendars tonight and get back to you about whether we can come."
- **The Counteroffer:** This is responding with an alternative that better fits your priorities as a couple. "We can't attend the event tonight at your house, but we would love to go on a walk with you some Saturday morning."[2]

When it comes to the difficult nos—to setting boundaries with thirds—things get more complicated. These situations require a greater degree of caution, care, and vigilance. With thirds, after all, it's easy to get out of sync with your partner and end up in a major conflict. Your brother's or friend's or mother-in-law's request can easily divide the two of you and pit you against each other. So the tactics here are slightly more complex:

- **Step 1: Always buy time.** When it comes to difficult thirds, it's never a good idea to make a big decision without first talking to your partner. In fact, that's how a third can exert the most outside influence on your system. So when a tough invitation, request, or demand surfaces, the first response is "Let us talk about it and we'll get back to you."
- **Step 2: Have a shared-success conversation.** By buying time, you and your partner now have the space to have a conversation about the following question: "What's best for [insert your team name]?"
- **Step 3: Stick together.** When you do finally say no and set the boundary, stay on the same team. The worst thing you can do with a difficult third is to present a divided front—to say, "You know, I really wanted to come this weekend, but my wife just wasn't that interested." That's yet another break in your system that can lead to drama.

Whether it's an easy or hard no, the goal is the same—to courageously set the boundaries that allow you to live your priorities.

The Freedom in Living on the Other Side of No

Geoff Smart understands the challenge of setting boundaries as well as anyone. He's a bestselling author and one of the most sought-after experts in the world on business hiring strategy. Each day, he receives hundreds of emails and calls with enticing offers, requests for help, and desperate pleas for a quick conversation. Geoff and his wife, Lauren, also have seven children. And that leaves him with a dilemma. Either he can say yes to everything coming his way, which would result in less time with his wife and kids. Or he can set a boundary and say no so that he can live up to his A priority in life: spending time with his family.

As an expert in human behavior, Geoff knew it wasn't as simple as saying he was going to prioritize his family. He had to build a system of checks, balances, and reminders to turn this aspiration into a reality. As he explained to us, "Most people in the business world live with the idea that if the system needs to flex, it's going to flex in the direction of spending more time on business. I decided to do the opposite. I have set up my family time so that it is fixed. So if the system gets overloaded, the amount of time I spend with my family stays the same. My time at the office is what gets compromised."

To pull off this countercultural feat, Geoff and Lauren have a dedicated family calendar, in which time with each other and family time are blocked and untouchable. They also both made difficult structural decisions in their careers to free up more time for being together as a family. Once they placed a priority on time together as a family and as a couple, in other words, they changed the structure of their lives and set clear boundaries to protect it.

In contrast to the "You can have it all" motto, they are also clear that there are real trade-offs that come with these boundaries—that prioritizing one area of life means other areas will be impacted negatively. As Geoff told us, "These kinds of decisions aren't easy. You have to come to grips with the fact that you will make less money and you will accomplish fewer things in your career if you prioritize your family like this. That's just the physics of it."

Couples like Geoff and Lauren have designed their life with boundaries that allow them to prioritize time with each other and time with their kids over everything else. That's their A in life. You and your partner's design for shared success, by contrast, may rest on different values that require different boundaries and priorities.

The real lesson we learn from couples like Geoff and Lauren isn't *what* to prioritize, it's *how* to prioritize. To design a life together that reflects your highest priorities, you have to set boundaries, you have to say no, and you may even have to accept that your boundaries come with real trade-offs—that you can't have it all. You may miss out on amazing business opportunities. You may piss off some of your friends and family members. You may even lose some relationships in the process.

This isn't easy and it isn't always fun. But consider the alternative. Imagine what it would be like to say to each other, "Let's take that two-week road trip to Alaska that we've always dreamed about," and then never do it. Imagine what it would be like to tell your child, "We are going to make it to all your soccer games this year," and then not show up to a single one. Imagine what it would be like to say to each other, "This year, we are going to make exercise a top priority," and then stop working out after the second week of January, all because you are too busy and have too much to do. In fact, you probably don't even have to imagine what this would be like because you've most likely done it. We certainly have.

To varying degrees, we have all compromised the things that matter most because we can't quite muster the courage or presence of mind to set clear boundaries. In modern life, saying yes when we really mean no has become one of our most destructive cultural habits. The momentum of life is too strong to just start saying no and stop saying yes. What we need is a more structured approach to protecting our shared values, along with clear boundaries and commitments.

We recommend an approach that begins with thinking of marriage like a boat. Just as you can sink a boat by overloading it with cargo, you can sink even the best marriage by getting caught in this habit of living without boundaries, of saying yes when you really mean no. To protect the things that matter most in your relationship, you will now have the opportunity to reflect carefully on what you want to keep on your marriage boat and what needs to be thrown off the decks and into the sea.

What's on Your Boat?

This practice is an invitation to think about your shared life like a boat. The exercise breaks down into two parts. In part one, you will draw all the things you carry on your current boat. In part two, you will draw only the things that remain after thinking carefully about what you need, what you don't, and where you want to set some new boundaries with life.

Step 1: What's on your boat today?

Take a few minutes with your partner to draw (or write out) all the things you carry as a couple in your current relationship boat. You can also draw them to scale or draw boxes around them to indicate how much or how little of your time and energy they consume. Check out the following list for examples of events, activities, and commitments that you might want to include on your boat:

Career	Self-care	Aging parents
Spiritual/religious practice	Reading	Gardening/yard work
Couple friends	Learning new things	Screen time
Individual friends	Experiences	TV/movie watching
Time with parents	Hobbies	Time in nature
Family trips	Events	Alone time
Other trips	Community obligations	Rest time
Sports	Kids' activities	Sleep
Finances	Cooking	Coaching/therapy
Investments	Gift obligations	Personal growth

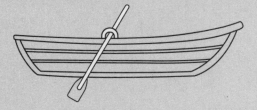

Now take a few minutes to debrief with your partner:

- Where do you have too much of something?
- Where do you have too little of something?
- What would you be better off throwing off the boat?

Tip 1: Shared success

Think back to your values of shared success to help guide these decisions.

Tip 2: Radical generosity

As you navigate this conversation, keep coming back—again and again and again—to the 80/80 mindset.

Step 2: What's on your dream boat?

Now you get to be bold. To actually live out your priorities together, what would your "dream boat" look like? What would be left on your boat if you fearlessly reduced or threw overboard the commitments, activities, people, or projects that threaten to sink your system? Here again, draw or list your commitments to scale.

Step 3: What three to five boundaries with life would the two of you have to set to turn this dream boat into a reality?

This is your opportunity to transform the insights from this exercise into changes in real life. With your partner, come up with actionable boundaries you could set right now or sometime this week to keep your marriage boat from sinking.

Boundary 1: _____

Boundary 2: _____

Boundary 3: _____

Boundary 4: _____

Boundary 5: _____

Hopefully, you now have a better sense of what to say no to in order to live out your priorities of shared success. Now comes the hard part: actually setting these boundaries. As you do this, it can be helpful to remember two things. First, boundaries are the key to living out your values of shared success. Second, while you may encounter resistance along the way, many people will ultimately respect you for making these hard decisions in service of your highest priorities as a couple.

CHAPTER 12

Power—Who's in Control?

Being in a band is a lot like being in a marriage. You spend most of your time together. You travel together. You occasionally argue and fight with each other. And just like in a marriage, you have to somehow figure out how to balance the dynamics of power that sit at the intersection of individual and shared success.

Take Freddie Mercury, the late lead singer of the British band Queen. For years, Freddie was the face of the band. At concerts, he took center stage in the spotlight. On album covers, he sat in the middle. And when it came to royalty checks, he took in far more than his fair share.

This wasn't some random accident. It was by design. Early on, Freddie came up with a simple rule that shaped the balance of power in the band for years. As the rock historian Mark Hodkinson explains, "Freddie announced, with his usual imperiousness, that he considered the 'writer' of a song to be the person who had contributed the lyric."[1] This may not sound like a big deal. But the writer of the song didn't just get the credit. He or she also earned half of the total royalties for the song, leaving the others to divide up the rest.

It's a system that worked out well for Freddie and guitarist Brian May, who wrote most of their early hits. But it didn't work out so well for drummer Roger Taylor and bassist John Deacon, who wrote fewer songs. It also didn't work out so well for the band itself. This rule created a band culture of competition, envy, and division. As Freddie admitted toward the end of his life, "The [songwriting] rule almost certainly discouraged us from co-operating on lyrics for a long time and started a trend towards separateness in song writing."[2]

Then, after almost twenty years of touring together, life happened. Freddie received a crushing diagnosis: he had HIV/AIDS. After he broke the news of his illness to the band, the members of Queen came to a joint decision: it was time to change the songwriting rule. They agreed to share the songwriting credits among everyone in the band. Looking back, Brian May said of this change, "I think Freddie and I squashed Roger and John in the beginning. We were the major songwriters and we didn't give them enough say. Now it's totally equal."[3]

The story of Queen is the story of how subtle structures of power can create massive ruptures in the spirit of shared success. In those early years, the band arranged power around individual success. They created a culture of "When I win, you lose," or in this case, "When my hit song skyrockets to the top of the charts, I get rich, you don't." When they changed this simple rule, however, the entire structure of power shifted toward shared success. They moved to a culture of "When I win, we all win."

The Many Faces of Power in Marriage

Marriage isn't exactly like being a rock star. But as we'll see, the dynamics of power work in many of the same ways. In marriage, as in rock and roll, organizing power around shared success changes everything.

So how does power show up in marriage? When power falls out of balance, you feel like you're being controlled by another person. And not just any person. You're being controlled and pushed around by the person you decided to spend the rest of your life with. It's the perfect setup for conflict and rage.

On top of all that, as we found in our interviews, many people feel embarrassed talking about power. We asked most couples how they experienced differences in power, and many of them initially dodged the question. They would say things like "Well, we're equals, so we don't really have to deal with that." And yet a minute or two later, they would share stories of a power play in which one person felt steamrolled, disrespected, or manipulated.

So the first step in understanding the power dynamics of marriage is to bring these dynamics out into the open—to begin to see them more clearly. To help illuminate the subtle inner workings of power, consider some examples.

Let's start with Ben. He out earned his former partner Shawn by a factor of five, which set up a toxic power dynamic that placed tremendous strain on their relationship. As Ben told us, "Money was the most stressful part of our relationship. We had a joint card and every time he used that card, *he* felt like he was taking from me. And that set up a dynamic where he had to defend himself from being a taker. Ultimately, that's what ended our relationship."

Then there's Michaela. In her relationship, she's consistently had the more prestigious job with the bigger salary. And as she reluctantly admitted to us, she catches herself using her status as the higher earner to exert just a little bit more clout than her partner: "When it comes to choosing where we go on vacation, that's always my choice. It's strange to say it out loud, but I really do think to myself, 'Well, I'm paying for the majority of the trip, so I'm going to pick where we go.'"

Or take Pete. He earned less than his spouse for the first few years of marriage. But then one day he sold his business, and in an instant, the balance of power changed. He told us, "When I started making more money, I felt a shift in power around how we talked about spending our money. I felt like I had more sway. One time when we were planning our budget I even said, 'This is my money,' and my wife quickly reminded me, 'No, it's not. This is *our* money.'"

Or consider Michelle. She's an owner of several hair salons who significantly out earns her husband: "I set up our system so that I would always have more power, and for some reason I've always been attracted to men who have less power than me." Michelle admitted that she both loves and hates having more power than her husband. "I really like the financial control that I have, but I realize it is preventing us from feeling more joy. And so I often wonder, 'Why don't I just loosen my grip on power for a moment and stop holding it over his head?'"

These are just a few of the ways power shows up in the marriages of others. But the real question is: How does it show up in your relationship? What are the conflicts that arise from an imbalance in control, decision rights, or financial resources?

These are questions worth considering as we begin to explore how to organize power in a more balanced way, around the idea of shared success.

The Invisible Force of Power in Marriage

So what is power anyway? We think of it as a structure of control that comes in two forms: balanced and imbalanced. Balanced power is what we're working toward in the 80/80 structure. It allows both partners to have a say, to push back, to share in making the big decisions, or to leave the relationship if things become unworkable. Balanced power includes checks, balances, and ways to participate, together, in meaningful decisions, all so that the system of marriage leads to shared success.

Imbalanced power, on the other hand, is what happens when these dynamics consistently favor the interests of one partner over the other. It's a system in which one partner has all the say, controls the other, makes the big decisions, or has the ability to discourage or even prevent the other from leaving. In its most insidious forms, it's a dynamic in which control of one partner over the other is arbitrary—in which the dominant partner effectively rules over the other in big and small ways.[4]

When you try to hide the cost of that expensive new mountain bike from your partner, the one with dual suspension and titanium components that weighs less than a Thanksgiving turkey, power is imbalanced. You just withheld vital information about your finances and took away their ability to fully understand or push back on your decision to make this major purchase.

When you never consult your partner and then tell them at the last minute that you're headed off to stay in a ski lodge with some old college friends for the weekend, power is imbalanced. You just took the decision of how to spend the weekend out of their hands, and even worse, you left them to manage everything while you're gone without really asking.

Here's the funny thing about power. From the outside, it often looks like one person holds all the power and the other is a kind of marital servant, tending to their partner's every whim. And it's true, there are 80/20 relationships in which this is the case. But more often than not, the power moves of one partner lead the other to push back with a move of their own.

We call it the *blowback rule*. And that's just a fancy way of saying that when you mess with your partner in the domain of power, they're going to mess with you back. Jim and Donna are a perfect example. When they decided to build a house during the birth of their second child, Jim ran the show. At the time, Donna was on bed rest in the hospital. So Jim picked the part of town. He picked the lot. And he came back to her saying, "Here's the survey. Just trust me. This is where we should build the house."

There was just one problem. The way this major life decision played out didn't sit well with Donna. She felt cut out of the process, as if this critical decision ended up being *his*, not at all *theirs*. So when the construction process for building their new house turned to putting the finishes on their new house, Donna took over. "Since he picked the location of the house and he's always traveling for work anyway," she thought, "I'm going to run the interior design my way." Now Jim took a back seat to the big decisions over countertops, furniture, light fixtures, and kitchen appliances. They set a budget, but Donna felt justified in overspending because this was her show, not Jim's. And besides, Jim hadn't consulted her in choosing where to build the house, so why should she consult him in finishing the construction?

This is the blowback rule in action. What we learn from Jim and Donna is that when power goes out of balance, each resulting move becomes like an act in a war that's impossible to win, one that leaves both partners living with some of the most uncomfortable emotions in all of married life: resentment, anger, fear, and rage. Because, let's face it, nobody likes to be pushed around and controlled in life. Nobody likes to be told what to do. And that's exactly what happens and how we feel when the dynamics of power go out of balance.

The research on power in relationships shows that men and women report having this experience of feeling subordinate to their partners in roughly equal numbers. And yet it also tells us that the cost of these power imbalances to women is higher. Psychologist Laina Bay-Cheng, for instance, found that low-power men don't really seem to care as much about asymmetrical power. They also experience almost no real cost of feeling less powerful than their spouse. For low-power women, by contrast, powerlessness comes at a much higher cost. Unlike low-power men, women report being more susceptible to coercion and even physical abuse by their spouse as a result of these dynamics.[5]

It's research that brings us back to a central theme of the 80/80 model. Against the backdrop of lingering 80/20 inequalities, just as men need to push their edge of radical generosity even further than women, men have a special responsibility to do their part (and more) in achieving a balanced dynamic of power in marriage.

The Power of Shared Success

How can we avoid these power struggles and rebalance power? It all comes back to the lessons of Freddie Mercury and Queen. A structure designed around self-interest and individual success quickly leads to imbalances in power. A structure designed around shared success, on the other hand, does the opposite. It creates a healthy balance of power that allows the relationship to thrive.

The best way to begin building this structure of shared success is to look at a few of the areas in marriage where we tend to fall out of balance. The first is money. The second is around the house. The third is sex.

The rest of this chapter explores the first two questions. We've devoted the next chapter to that last question of balancing power in the bedroom.

Financial Power—The Power of the Purse

Let's face it, we live in a world where money is perhaps the ultimate indicator of status and power. Those with lots of it have more sway in politics, media, and even ordinary, everyday conversations.

The same holds true in marriage. As we've seen, many couples fall into a dynamic in which the higher-earning spouse has a subtle but disproportionate influence over decisions big and small: where to go on vacation, whether to buy a new car, or whether to splurge on some extravagant personal expense. And the blowback rule tells us that when one partner exerts financial power, the other is going to push back, often in some entirely unrelated way.

This basic fact of modern life, however, doesn't mean that the goal should be to balance power by equalizing income. In our interviews, we found that couples with a balanced power structure often had radically different career paths with radically unequal incomes. Some were single-breadwinner families in which one spouse stayed home. Some were families in which one partner worked full time in a "big" job while the other worked part time.

We also observed dual-earning couples with similar incomes who slipped into these asymmetrical dynamics of power. Sure, they each brought in the same amount of money. But somehow, that didn't magically solve the power problem. There was something deeper going on, something that couldn't be fixed by making income equal.

What we learned is while money often creates imbalances in power, it's not necessarily the cure for these imbalances. Instead, the cure is to design a new structure of power dynamics around the goal of shared success—to manage money in a way that promotes rather than disrupts the experience of winning together.

How can you do that? Consider two core principles. One is about how you save your money as a couple. The other is about how you spend it.

Principle 1: Shared Success Means Shared Savings

This first principle is the most basic and also the most essential principle of marriage, money, and shared success.

To win together, you need to have some shared pot of resources.

This doesn't mean that you have to scrap your prenup (if you have one) and move everything into a single account. That works for some couples, but not all. What it does mean is that you need at least some shared pool of resources. To aspire toward shared success without actually sharing anything, after all, is like saying you want to donate to important causes without ever giving anything. It's a positive intention without real action.

When it comes to sharing financial resources, here are three primary models to consider:

- **All in:** If you want to go all the way with shared success, this is the model we recommend. In this model, everything is shared: bank accounts, investments, bills, debt, etc. The virtue of this model lies in its simplicity. By going all in, you're committing to shared every-thing, which is the perfect design for shared success.

- **Side stashes:** Some couples find that they each still want a small pot of money separate from their shared accounts, money that they can spend freely, without having to worry about how their partner might react. The best way to set this up is using what financial adviser Priya Malani calls a *side stash*—a small amount of money set aside for each person in his or her own separate account.[6] This system is like an allowance for adults. To set this model up, all you have to do is create a monthly auto-withdrawal from your joint account into these two individually held side stash accounts.

- **Separate finances with a joint stash:** Couples who still want to keep their finances separate can create a joint stash of shared re-sources. This strategy works like the side stash in reverse. Keep your individual accounts separate and then create a shared account in the name of your family team. You fund this account through monthly automatic withdrawals from each of your individual ac-counts. Either you can withdraw the same amount from both of your accounts, or if one of you makes more than the other, you can make the withdrawal amount proportional to income (for instance, if you each agree to contribute 5 percent each month to the joint pool, someone making $10,000 a month contributes $500, while someone making $1,000 a month contributes $50).

We strongly recommend the first two models, all in and side stash, because they are most closely aligned with the spirit of shared success. The more you share, after all, the easier it becomes to live out the core 80/80 belief: "When I win, you win."

But even if you can't make one of these two models work, you can still take steps toward arranging money and power in your marriage around shared success. The key is to make sure that you have at least some shared pool of funds—some way of ensuring that your win makes your partner financially better off and that their win does the same for you.

Principle 2: Create Structure Around Spending

The first principle is about how we save. The second is about how we spend.

Create a shared structure to guide spending decisions.

Why create a more structured approach to spending? It turns out that differences of opinion around spending lead to many of the nastiest conflicts in marriage. When one partner unilaterally buys a Jet Ski or a top-of-the-line Dyson vacuum cleaner, it can lead to an ugly push-and-pull of power that lasts for years.

Some couples get lucky on this one. They just happen to have similar attitudes on spending and rarely get caught in this financial struggle. For others, however, conflict over spending can become the central source of disagreement in marriage. They fight about one partner spending too much on a run to the grocery store: "Why do you have to buy seven-dollar organic almond butter, anyway?" They fight about one partner rolling into the driveway with a new motorcycle: "You're telling me that we don't have the money for a new washer and dryer and you just bought this?"

These fights can suck the air of connection out of even the heathiest marriages. The good news is that there's a relatively straightforward solution to this problem, one we learned from Charles and Rita, a couple well aware of just how explosive this struggle over spending can be. As Rita told us, "I see couples all the time where one partner, usually the wife, feels controlled by her husband, who has a higher income."

To solve this problem, Charles and Rita created a budget. At the beginning of each year, they meet and agree on how much they want to spend on various things. As Charles told us, "This is a budget that goes down to line items like my clothing, Rita's clothing, children's clothing, entertainment, home improvements, vacations, and Uber rides."

This exercise can be especially difficult for the higher-earning partner. It requires them to be reasonable and generous. They are, after all, likely putting more money into the pot. It also requires both partners to agree to live within the constraints of the budget.

And yet for Charles and Rita, the results have been life-changing. They don't fight about money. They don't worry about who makes more or who makes less. They don't have to because, as Charles observed, "By having a clear budget, no one feels controlled. We've both participated in the decision and agreed on how the money is going to be spent."

Sounds great in theory. But how do you put together a family budget built for shared success? The next practice is designed to help guide you through the process.

The Family Budget for Shared Success · 80/80 PRACTICE

If you and your partner experience conflict around power and spending, this exercise is for you. It's designed to get you started on creating a family budget for shared success.

Step 1: Go back to your values of shared success

Look at the financial implications of these values. If your goal is to travel more often, how much money do you need to do that? If your goal is to save up for a house, how much do you need for a down payment? Let these values—not your random spending habits—determine two key numbers: how much you want to save (and for what) and how much you want to spend on maintaining your life.

Step 2: Take a close look at your current spending

You just outlined a spending goal based on your shared values. Now it's worth seeing how close you are to it. To do that, use one of the many family financial tools available to generate a report of your current spending. If possible, calculate both total annual and monthly spending as well as annual and monthly spending within categories such as auto, clothing, groceries, dining out, entertainment, utilities, and travel.

Step 3: How do you need to change your spending?

This is the key question. To stay aligned with your values of shared success, what changes in spending do you need to make together? Here again, see if you can make these decisions from the spirit of shared success. Ask, "What changes in spending are best for us?"

Step 4: Write out a simple family budget

This doesn't have to be a complicated financial model. All you have to do is record your agreements around spending goals in a spreadsheet or other document. You can get as detailed as you want here, with specific budget targets for groceries, dining out, and personal expenses. Or you can keep it more general. A good rule of thumb, however, is the more conflict you have around money, the more detailed you want to make this budget.

Tip 1: Navigating conflict

What if one of you disregards the budget and overspends on clothes, sports equipment, fishing trips, or patio furniture? Moments like these are the perfect opportunity for the Reveal and Request practice. It's an invitation to talk openly about what happened and then adjust the structure of the budget if needed.

Tip 2: The 80/80 mind

This one goes without saying by now: radical generosity, always.

Domestic Power—Influence and Control
at the Kitchen Counter

The power of money influences everything. And yet money isn't the only form of power in marriage. The day-to-day hum of life is also shaped by power over things like coordinating the social calendar, taking time away from the family to be with friends or family members, mapping out your kids' playdates and camp calendar, carving out space for self-care activities, planning how many trips you will take (To where? When? And for how long?), as well as countless other seemingly trivial areas of daily life. Just like financial power, the way we carry out these ordinary tasks can lead to either shared success or imbalances in power that lead to conflict and resentment.

What does the domestic struggle for power look like? First, there's the struggle for logistical control. This is what happens when one partner makes a decision that impacts the entire family without consulting the other. If you create plans and just assume your partner's job is to work around you while also taking care of the rest of life's demands—cooking meals, walking the dog, childcare, calling the plumber—you're exerting logistical control. Your partner might push back by unilaterally inviting extended family to stay in the guest room for a week or setting up social events on weekends, all without ever consulting you—another logistical control move.

There's also the struggle for control over basic facts and information, often exerted by concealing important information from the other person. This form of domestic power sometimes manifests in subtle, seemingly harmless ways. When you know your partner hates baseball and wouldn't want to plan the day around a game you want to watch, so you subtly influence the schedule of events on a Sunday to ensure that your family magically returns home at two p.m., just in time for the start of the first inning, you're exploiting this form of control. You're getting your way by hiding your true intent. This form of power can also take on more extreme forms that have the potential to tear apart the fabric of trust in marriage. When you hide the cost of the clothes you bought from your partner by using a separate credit card, or when you hide the fact that you had coffee with an ex from college, you're concealing essential information from your partner. And worse, your partner has no idea it's even happening.

Finally, there's the struggle for control over household tasks. You might be thinking, "Who wants to control housework? Isn't the whole battle for fairness about getting the other person to take over more control?" But this power struggle surfaced over and over in our conversations with couples. Many over-contributing partners complain about doing so much around the house while subconsciously clinging to control over these tasks. One woman, for instance, told us that her husband feels it's unfair that he does so much work coordinating babysitters and housecleaners, but he's also unwilling to cede control and let her take over. As she put it, "When my husband feels it's unfair, I tell him that he can't just complain. He also has to relinquish control over the task to me, knowing that I might not be as good at it. And so far, he's unwilling to do that."

In the end, these three domestic power moves are really just about control. What's the remedy for these power imbalances? It's the same as the remedy for imbalances in money: Reorganize the structure of life around shared success. Collaborate when scheduling important events or making important decisions. Reveal the full truth with your spouse. Sometimes, it may even involve inviting your partner to learn how to take on some of the tasks in marriage that you currently control.

It's worth pointing out that letting go of domestic control is a lot like shifting from fairness to radical generosity. It can be unnerving, scary, and uncomfortable. And yet this letting-go sets the stage for a more balanced structure of shared success.

To give you a taste of this experience, we've designed a practice called the Power Swap. It's an invitation to begin loosening your grip on control (wherever you might be holding on to it). It's a chance to see for yourself if this move toward shared control and shared success helps dissolve the struggle for power at home.

The Power Swap

Ready for an 80/80 experiment? This practice gives you a way to see the dynamics of power in your relationship more clearly. It also provides an opportunity to experience what it would be like to let go of your areas of power and control in everyday life.

Step 1: Identifying power areas

Here are some areas where power imbalances often arise: family calendar management, logistics, childcare, kids' activities, financial planning, expense tracking, household management. You can even consider more emotional forms of power, such as starting conversations, compromising, attentiveness, listening, or initiating sex. Take a moment to consider where your partner holds more power and write these areas out in the chart below.

Tip: If you're feeling stuck

Think about what would happen if your partner suddenly vanished. What tasks would you have trouble managing or taking over? Which events would no longer happen? What skills would you need to learn? These are likely the areas where he or she holds more power.

PARTNER 1 Areas where my partner has more power than I do	PARTNER 2 Areas where my partner has more power than I do
Power Area 1:	Power Area 1:
Power Area 2:	Power Area 2:
Power Area 3:	Power Area 3:
Power Area 4:	Power Area 4:
Power Area 5:	Power Area 5:

Step 2: Pick a power area to swap

Have a conversation with your partner and pick a domain where you could try out a power swap for a weekend. This involves taking over the roles and responsibilities in one of your partner's domains. If you choose your partner's power around social planning, for example, the power swap makes you the social planner for the weekend.

Tip 1: Avoid highly contentious areas

No need to fight over this one. Keep it fun and maybe even funny.

Tip 2: Make it easy

Pick something that you could easily swap for a few days.

Tip 3: Radical generosity

Don't forget—your attitude is everything. See if you can do this experiment as an expression of love and an opportunity for growth. Be so radically generous that it hurts.

At the end of the weekend, have a conversation with your partner about the practice. What did you learn? What was it like to let go of control? How could you reduce these power imbalances going forward?

Want a More Advanced Practice?

Make one or more of these power swaps permanent.

This practice of balancing power in marriage and the other structural practices of shared success (roles, priorities, and boundaries) may not sound like the path to amazing intimacy. But now that we've explored these more tactical elements of the 80/80 structure, we're ready for the final chapter on shared success, one that focuses on what is perhaps the most wild, exciting, and potentially explosive area of married life: sex.

CHAPTER 13

Sex–Orgasmic Altruism

Blake sat at his desk in his dorm room, reviewing his notes for the next day's Human Biology midterm. It seemed like this was going to be just like any other ordinary Tuesday night. That is, until he heard the old-school *ding* of his AOL Instant Messenger. He looked up at his computer screen:

> Samantha027: What are u up to?

Samantha and Blake had been dating for six months now, since the beginning of their junior year in college. He typed back:

> BlakeDogg4: Just studying for Hum Bio. Want to hang out?
> Samantha027: Yes! Hike up to the satellite dish behind
> campus?

Thirty minutes later, sometime around eleven p.m., they parked their bikes and welcomed each other with a kiss. They approached the gate to the trailhead. It was locked and covered with signs reading, NO TRESPASSING. NO LOITERING. GROUNDS CLOSED AFTER DARK.

Samantha scaled the fence first. Blake followed. They hiked together up a winding trail through an open meadow lit by moonlight. When they finally made it up to the top of the hill, they found a spot off the trail where they could lie down and gaze up at the stars.

The view that night was unforgettable. And so was the sex.

Then there was that time in their late twenties. Six years into marriage, Blake and Samantha decided to take an anniversary trip to Cozumel. They spent their days together walking on the beach, sleeping in late, and exploring the island.

On their last night, they walked a half mile down the road to a small tiki-themed dance club on the beach. They rarely danced at home. They rarely stayed out late at a club. But tonight was different. Time disappeared. The music, the view, the warm ocean breeze, and their connection that night were amazing. And so was the sex.

Then there was last night. Now thirteen years into marriage, Blake and Samantha are the parents of two boys. Samantha had just returned home from a business trip to Chicago. Blake had spent the afternoon shuttling their two kids from school to soccer practice to trumpet lessons, all while taking conference calls from the sidelines of the soccer field and sending emails in the music school waiting room.

With so much going on, at five p.m., Blake texted Samantha, "Should we bail on date night?" She texted back, "Too late to cancel on the babysitter."

At nine thirty p.m., after drinks and dinner, with both kids in bed, they turned to each other. Blake mumbled sheepishly, "So are we going to, you know?"

Samantha took a deep breath. "I'm sorry, babe. It's just that I can barely keep my eyes open."

"It's been two weeks since the last time we had sex," Blake protested.

"All right, let's just do this," said Samantha.

Ten minutes later, they were both sound asleep.

With so much stress, so much to do, and so little time to do it in, their connection that night was only OK. And so was the sex.

What's Really Keeping Us Apart

Blake and Samantha aren't real people. They're a composite couple, built from the real challenges shared by the couples as well as the marriage and sex therapists we interviewed. The struggle they face is the same as the struggle many couples face. It's the challenge of holding on to the spark of intimacy in the midst of the sheer chaos of modern family life.

During the early years of a relationship, sex is often amazing. It spans the spectrum from dopamine-induced lust sex, in which you ravish each other, to transcendent sex, in which you take an ecstatic spiritual journey together into altered states of love, connection, desire, and the raw experience of becoming one together.

But then life happens. The dopamine wears off. The reality of living together sets in. You might even bring a kid or three into the picture. And somehow, sex can become just another to-do. It becomes "check-the-box" sex. This style of sex is what we often heard about from exhausted parents, hard-driving two-career couples, and others overwhelmed by the demands of modern life. And yet the fact that so many couples fall into this intimacy rut isn't some sort of marital failure. It's just what happens when we're so beaten down by work at the office, work at home, parenting, and the never-ending logistics of life that there's nothing left for intimacy.

And yet it doesn't have to be this way.

So here's the big question: Why does the experience of sex often change so dramatically in marriage? How is it possible that this most sensual and pleasurable of all human activities veers so quickly from lust or transcendence to just another box to check?

The easy answer, peddled to us by glossy magazines with airbrushed models on the covers, is that this is a sex problem. If we just had the right technique, used the right toys, or acted out the right role-play, sex would go back to being just like it was in the early days, instantly turning from mundane to mind-blowing.

There's only one problem with this conventional view: its assumption that sex is somehow separate from the rest of life in a committed relationship. The idea that it's a sex problem assumes that the way things go in the bedroom has almost nothing to do with the way things went in the kitchen yesterday morning, on the way home from the office, or at the hug-and-go line at school. It's this assumption that leads to the strange and yet widely held idea that the only thing holding you and your partner back from awesome sex is a Kama Sutra class, cherry-flavored Orgasm Balm, or a purple silicone vibrator shaped like a bunny rabbit.

If we learned anything from talking with other couples, as well as sex experts and sex therapists, it's that this conventional view is quite simply false. It's impossible to seal off what happens in the bedroom, during our most intimate moments, from the rest of life. Far from being separate, sex is more like the mirror of married life. Either it reflects the strength of your connection, or it reflects past resentments, misunderstandings, and wounds. As Corey Allan, a marriage and family therapist we interviewed, put it, "How you do life is how you do sex. How you do sex is how you do life."

The Life Challenges That Become Sex Challenges

If most couples don't have a sex problem, then what's turning the euphoric rapture of sex into just another mandatory to-do? There isn't one single smoking-gun problem responsible for a lackluster sex life. Rather, there are four complex, interconnected problems keeping those of us in established relationships from experiencing the joyful sex of our earlier years.

Time Scarcity

Most of us spend our days in a constant state of doing. We're always busy with something: getting the kids ready for school, firing off emails late at night in bed on our phones, or cramming work into every five-minute window that presents itself during the day. As a result, we have no space in life, no time left over at the end of the day or, for that matter, in any part of the day.

We're not just experiencing a shortage of white space on the calendar. We're also experiencing a shortage of mental space. All this doing, all the time spent rushing around and glued to our devices leaves us in a scattered frame of mind—a paradoxical state of feeling both wired and tired, in which our minds never seem to stop spinning.

This "always-on" state of doing and its accompanying lack of headspace effectively destroy the desire to have sex. The experience of eroticism, after all, requires the opposite. Amazing sex requires an abundance of time and space. It's at odds with the rushed pace and overstimulated mindset of the modern work-obsessed world. As Esther Perel, one of the world's leading experts on sex, puts it, "Eroticism is inefficient. It loves to squander time and resources."[1]

This pattern is a modern epidemic. The percentage of people having sex once a week dropped from 45 percent in 2000 to 36 percent in 2016.[2] Other research on sex in marriage shows a steady decline in sexual frequency within marriages and committed relationships during this same period, leading some to call our current age a "sexual recession."[3] Whether you're a teenager, single, married, or dating, the statistics say you're now having significantly less sex than you might have had twenty years ago, in the pre-smartphone age.

The point here is simply that we're having less sex because we're too busy and distracted to invest in the inefficient yet exquisite experience of making love to each other.

Unrevealed Resentment

The hurried pace of modern life isn't the only thing to blame for this lack of sexual desire. As we've seen throughout this book, the mindset and structure of the 50/50 model also wreaks havoc on sexual intimacy. If we're constantly keeping a mental tally of who contributed more, who cares more, and who's trying harder, we exist in a perpetual state of irritation and resentment. Our boundaries and priorities aren't clear. And on top of all that, we most likely have a mountain of emotional issues that we've never revealed or even discussed with each other.

What results from this mindset and the chaotic structure of life is a lingering sense of resentment that ebbs and flows but never fully goes away. It's there when you wake up. It's there when you see each other at the end of the day. Most important, it's there when you start taking each other's clothes off. The resentment toward your partner that you feel in life doesn't just magically disappear in the bedroom. In fact, it's often amplified there, which further dampens any remaining flames of sexual desire.

Consider Katrina. She told us that handling resentment and conflict turned out to be the key to unlocking a more vibrant sex life with her husband. "Because we've had this rigorous hygiene about cleaning up our conflicts," she observed, "we've always had a very active sex life and still do. And it's funny because I hear people saying all the time that when you've been together for more than ten years the sex just gets uninteresting. And I'm like 'Well, speak for yourself.'" What we learn from Katrina and her husband is that revealing the inevitable resentments that arise in married life is essential for opening to greater intimacy.

Power Struggle

We already know that money and power go together. The same is true of power and sex.

In fact, navigating power in the bedroom can be one of the messiest challenges in marriage. It's a challenge that often comes down to this: one partner wants it but the other doesn't. It sounds so simple. And yet this disconnect in sex drive brings up all sorts of sensitive and complicated dynamics of power.

From the perspective of the high-drive partner—the partner who generally wants to have more sex—this dynamic creates frustration and hurt feelings. Each time their advance is met with a no, they feel the sting of rejection. It's a feeling that may cause them to retreat—to just stop initiating altogether. Or it may cause them to act out—to lash out at their partner in seemingly unrelated ways or seek pleasure elsewhere in the form of porn or, in extreme cases, an affair.

From the perspective of the low-drive partner, however, it's just as complicated, if not more so. One woman told us, "When I say no to my husband, I feel guilt first, like I'm doing something wrong. But then I feel outraged. I think to myself, 'It's not my job to put out for you.'" This dynamic gets even more complicated when you layer in the historical baggage of traditional gender roles. When the man has the higher drive and the woman has the lower, you're now also working with the weight of centuries of sexual oppression directed at women.

It's a complicated dynamic that leaves the higher-drive partner playing the role of initiator and the lower-drive partner playing the role of gatekeeper. Both roles hold power. The initiator exerts power through their advances. And yet the gatekeeper also exerts power. As one woman told us of this dynamic, "Sex can easily be used as a weapon, a tool of power. I was always the gatekeeper when it came to sex. Because I had the lower drive, I always decided whether we were going to do it."

This is a problem with a fancy technical name in the field of psychology:

sexual desire discrepancy, or SDD. Research suggests that over the course of any given month, 80 percent of people in long-term relationships will experience some sort of desire discrepancy with their partner. The research also suggests that disagreements over desire discrepancy can be extremely destabilizing and difficult to resolve.[4]

Mismatched Expectations

One of our most fascinating conversations about sex in marriage was with a Christian sex blogger who goes under the pseudonym J. Parker. She started her blog, *Hot, Holy and Humorous*, after growing up in a Christian household where the overriding message about sex was quite simply: DON'T. In her words, "Don't do it, don't talk about it, don't even think about it." Once she got married, J. Parker realized she had no idea how to think about sex. She also realized she wasn't alone—that many Christian women were also struggling with these mixed messages about sex.

We asked her where she sees couples running into problems about sex. She mentioned lack of connection. She mentioned the power struggles we just explored. But she also mentioned the problem of mismatched expectations around sex. As she explained, "What I see is that porn and erotica has changed what we expect from our partner. You get the sense from it that everyone's available to have sex at any moment. We've created a culture of unrealistic expectations."

There's a growing body of evidence to support these concerns about the impact of porn on romantic relationships.[5] But the problem here cuts deeper. The real problem is that our expectations around sex often don't match our partner's. One partner might approach sex with the expectation that it should be wild, loud, and maybe even a bit raunchy sometimes. Meanwhile, the other partner might approach it with the expectation of being held, not groped; loved, not tied up.

The real problem, however, isn't so much that we have different expectations—that's to be expected when dealing with something as taboo as sex. The real problem is that so many couples find it difficult to talk openly about these expectations. It's not wrong to like it wild. It's not wrong to like it gentle. It's not wrong to have crazy fantasies. But it starts to feel that way when we can't talk about it openly. What results is a disconnect that, like all the others, pushes couples further apart and makes satisfying sex that much more elusive.

It All Comes Down to Connection

If there's a single theme running throughout these four barriers to sex, it's lack of connection. In their own way, all of these problems pull us further apart. And the further we drift apart, the less turned on we feel.

Why does connection either open or close the door to amazing sex? Sex is the most sacred, raw, naked, and exposed of all marital acts. The moment we take off all our clothes and merge together, there's no hiding behind anything. We're connected in the most profound and intimate of ways.

Without deep emotional connection, there's an unconscious urge to avoid getting this close. In this state of disconnection, it feels better to go on Facebook than to experience the openness and vulnerability of making love. It's safer to watch TV or work at all hours of the night and day than it is to seduce your partner all the way to the bedroom.

When connection deepens, however, this emotional barrier starts to fade. Sex emerges as a natural expression of love and connection. You don't want to surf random blogs or BuzzFeed articles as you lie next to your partner in bed. You want to roll over and hold them. You don't want to spend your evenings getting to in-box 0. You would rather have amazing sex with this person you love.

The 80/80 Guide to Getting It On

Sustaining a meaningful sex life beyond those dopamine-fueled early years of marriage isn't easy. It requires real work. And yet it also pays out huge rewards. Sex is the ultimate expression of connection and love. It helps us stay close, in sync, and caring for each other. Not to mention the fact that when things are working well, sex is one of the most fun, pleasurable, and spiritually sublime things you can do in all of life.

So it's worth thinking carefully about how to allow this most sacred act to flourish. In the 80/80 marriage, we've found that there are two key steps to finding your way back to amazing sex. Step one is solving the life-related problems that get in the way of getting it on. Step two is addressing the sex-related problems, such as asymmetrical dynamics of power and mismatched expectations.

Step 1: Solving the Life-Related Problems

How can you shift the mindset and structure of life to deepen your connection with your partner and have better sex? The answer should be clear by now. It's everything we've been exploring in this book. It's the 80/80 model.

This model gives us the mindset, structure, and tools to address all the life-related problems that can keep us from experiencing better sex. Consider the first problem, time scarcity—the busyness of modern life and its accompanying lack of mental space for intimacy. Books on sex in marriage offer all sorts of solutions to the problem of time scarcity, like having a date night once a week or, as Esther Perel recommends, creating unbounded space together, say, from Friday evening to the next morning, or an entire weekend, so you can drop off the grid of doing, get a little crazy like you did in your younger years, and let the inefficient yet ecstatic experience of erotic sex organically emerge.[6]

These tips are fantastic. And yet actually doing them is impossible without addressing two deeper structural issues we explored earlier in the book: a lack of clear priorities and the inability to set clear boundaries.

The fact that we're too busy to have amazing sex isn't some inevitable glitch of modern life. It's a priorities problem. As a culture, we have prioritized completion over connection, doing over being together. The key to reversing this pattern is to make time together as a couple a higher priority—to arrange your life around a value that says, "If forced to choose between finishing up those final work tasks and lying in bed doing nothing of productive value together, we choose the latter."

Priorities remind us of the priceless value of sex and connection. Boundaries protect this value. Agreeing you won't use smartphones or tablets in bed—that's a boundary that protects intimacy. Agreeing to avoid spending all of date night talking through logistics—that's another boundary designed to protect the space of intimacy. Agreeing to stop working and meet each other in bed at nine p.m.—that's yet another intimacy-promoting boundary.

Then there's the second life-related sex problem: the sexual buzzkill of unrevealed resentments. From the perspective of the 80/80 model, the best way to unwind resentment in the bedroom is to unwind it in *all* of life so that sex mirrors a life lived from a place of radical generosity and a structure of shared success. To unwind resentment in life, we can again turn to the tools of the 80/80 model. Instead of keeping score and viewing everything your partner does with a mindset of fairness, shift to the mindset of radical generosity. Instead of avoiding difficult conversations and skipping over expressing hard truths to your partner, give your marriage the gift of a clean Reveal and Request that allows you to get back in sync. Instead of allowing your accidental habits to create a structure of chaos and confusion, shift to clear roles and structures of shared success that make you feel more like a team.

These are the shifts that lead to connection in life. And as we have seen, connection in even the most trivial corners of life—washing dishes, buying butter at the store, or picking up your kid from a piano lesson—translates to connection in the bedroom. And that in turn translates to better sex.

The research on sex in marriage supports this surprising connection between how we handle life logistics and how we hook up in the bedroom. Sociologist Daniel L. Carlson, for example, found that couples with balanced power structures have more and better sex than traditional 80/20 couples or couples in which the woman over-contributes. In these more balanced relationships, he observes, "This isn't, 'You do your thing, and I'll do my thing.' It requires cooperation, good communication and good coordination. And that builds strong bonds."[7]

That's why the seemingly unsexy mindset and structure of the 80/80 model matter. It's why sex follows chapters about the logistics and structure of married life. Reflecting on roles, priorities, boundaries, and power might not elicit erotic desire, at least not right away. But streamlining your structure of life allows you to spend less time lost in the chaos, drama, and resentment of life's logistical challenges and more time feeling close and connected to your spouse. And when that happens, the research and good old-fashioned common sense tell us, you're far more likely to want to seduce your partner.

One final point. We don't want to sell you on a false ideal here. The other insight we gleaned from interviewing couples about their sex lives is that even the most connected partners have dry spells or periods of check-the-box sex. Sex isn't an experience you can control or design with perfect precision. It's more like a creative work of art. Sometimes it's spectacular. Sometimes it's really good. Sometimes it's not great. That's just the way of it.

When connection is deep, however, most couples report that they spend less time checking boxes and more time experiencing powerful states of pleasure and love.

WHAT'S YOUR 80/80 PATH TO BETTER SEX?

By now, it should be clear that the way you handle the ordinary logistics of life shapes your experience in the bedroom. So before moving on, it can be helpful to reflect with your partner on the following question: Which 80/80 practice has the greatest potential to improve your sex life?

Each couple will likely have a different answer. It could be setting clearer boundaries so you actually have time and space for intimacy. It could be unwinding power dynamics so you feel less resentment and more desire. It could be getting clearer on roles so you stop nagging each other and fighting over who took out the trash. Or it could be a mindset shift such as practicing radical generosity or appreciation, or revealing issues as they arise.

Step 2: Solving the Sex-Related Problems

Now consider the two problems more closely related to sex itself. The first is the problem of power struggles in the bedroom, one that stems from the differences between each partner's levels of sexual desire.

How can you bring greater balance to sex and power? The answer is similar to the one we offered when talking about power and money in the previous chapter. When one partner holds the power to dictate how you spend your money, the solution is to add a little structure—to neutralize the power of the high earner by creating an agreed-upon budget.

The same principles apply to balancing out the power of the high-drive and low-drive partner. Put simply, the key is to add a little bit of structure and radical generosity to the decision around whether to have sex.

ENDING THE SEX POWER STRUGGLE

Here are four strategies for dissolving the power struggle around sex.

STRATEGY 1: SCHEDULING SEX

For many couples, the very idea of scheduling sex sounds like the ultimate erotic buzzkill. Sex, after all, should be spontaneous, impulsive, and in the moment. It shouldn't be reduced to yet another meeting on the calendar. But scheduling time for sex doesn't have to take the erotic edge off it. This isn't about sending a fifteen-minute "Let's screw" invite. It's about setting up longer blocks of time that open a space for erotic moments to organically emerge. It might be a full hour or two reserved for connection. It's a long hike that returns to an empty house. If you have even more flexibility, it can be a date night with no end time or a weekend away from the kids. Think of it less like scheduling a business meeting and more like making time to have an affair with your spouse.

STRATEGY 2: THE SEX CHALLENGE

Tony and Alisa DiLorenzo, authors of *7 Days of Sex Challenge*, introduced us to this idea.[8] It's the idea of scrambling your ordinary habits around sex by doing it every day for a week, a month, or even a year. Tony and Alisa decided to try it because they were losing connection. So they went for it by doing a sixty-day challenge—an audacious experiment that they credit as having saved their marriage.

They've since learned that even a one-week sex challenge has a similar effect. The reason? As Alisa told us, "Because sex was on the table every day, it was no longer a weapon of power. There was no longer a battle over 'Do I want to?' or 'Do I not want to?' And it forced us to start connecting again."

STRATEGY 3: ORGASMIC ALTRUISM

This practice unites sex and radical generosity as a way to dissolve the power struggle. Think of it as orgasmic altruism. One woman told us that this application of radical generosity to sex changed her marriage: "I made an intentional commitment to meet his sexual energy. For my husband, there was an intentional commitment to dial it back so that he could meet mine. We both moved toward each other because it's such a fundamental way of staying connected."

She is describing the 80/80 rule applied to sex. It's moving beyond the line of fairness, which stops at 50 percent. For the high-drive partner, this means being gentler around initiating sex, adjusting to a less frequent rhythm, and being generous when you receive a no. For the low-drive partner, this might mean being more open to the possibility of your partner getting you in the mood, even if you're not at the outset. Or it might mean asking, "Why am I not in the mood?" and revealing any lingering issues or resentments so you can come back into connection. In short, orgasmic altruism is leaning toward each other in the realm of sexual desire out of a spirit of generosity.

STRATEGY 4: TURNING REJECTION INTO A SEX PLAN

No matter what you do, there will be times when one person wants to have sex and the other doesn't. In these cases, there are two ways to say no. The first is a simple no: "Not tonight, honey. I'm not in the mood." It's a no that feels like a pure rejection to the partner receiving it. The second is to say no and then offer another time when you might want to have sex. It sounds like this, "I'm exhausted tonight, but let's do it tomorrow night."

Sounds subtle. But for the higher-drive partner, this second response can change everything. It softens the bite of rejection. It also takes away the uncertainty that comes with receiving a pure no to sex. It puts an end to thoughts like "Does this mean we're not going to have sex all week, all month, all year?"

Which of these strategies might work best to enhance your sex life? We recommend having a conversation about this question and then experimenting with the strategies that resonate most with the two of you.

Revealing Your Expectations Around Sex

Now for the final sex-related problem: mismatched expectations. This may seem like a new problem, a dilemma that's outside the framework of the 80/80 model. But when we look more closely, it's really just a sex-related revealing problem that goes back to the core insights of chapter seven, in which we looked at how best to deal with the potholes and sinkholes that arise in marriage.

Just as it's often difficult to reveal misunderstandings or hurt feelings in life, many couples find it difficult to talk openly about sex. It's hard to ask for what you really want in the bedroom. It's easier to just keep doing what you've been doing for years. It's risky to share a new fantasy that you want to explore. It's easier to pretend things are going great. It's really hard to tell your partner that what they're doing doesn't feel good to you. But these difficult conversations are the key to increasing your sexual satisfaction.

Just like unrevealed emotional issues, unexpressed expectations in sex create slow and subtle ruptures in connection. With each microscopic unspoken truth, the divide grows. Connection fades. And sex slowly turns into yet another chore.

The solution to the mismatched expectations problem is the same as the solution in the revealing chapter. It may not be fun. You may feel fear or irritation. But see what happens when you push yourself out of your comfort zone and begin sharing your desires, preferences, fantasies, and expectations around sex with your partner.

Opening up this conversation around sex can be quite difficult for many couples, especially those who have spent years avoiding the subject. So for some couples, it's helpful to add a bit more structure. Instead of just revealing issues or requests when they arise, it can be helpful to explore the following questions together.

Let's (Finally) Talk About Sex

80/80
PRACTICE

Use these questions to open up the conversation around sex. As you take turns answering each question, remember to speak and listen with a spirit of radical generosity.

Tip 1: Pick the right time

If done right, talking about sex together often leads to a surge in connection and sexual energy. So save this conversation for a date night or some other time when you and your partner can easily transition into sex.

Tip 2: Radical generosity

Make it sexy this time.

Now for the questions:

How can I know you're interested in having sex?

Is there anything I do during foreplay or sex that turns you off?

What do I do during foreplay or sex that turns you on or that you want me to do more of?

Do you have any fantasies that you want to try out together?

Talk me through your favorite, most unforgettable memory of us having sex.

Imagine you could create the most amazing, mind-blowing night of sex. What would it look like?

Want a More Advanced Practice?

Turn that last question from imagination to reality.

Use your answers as a blueprint to create an unforgettable night together.

There's one last point we want to make about sex. We are not sex experts, and this isn't a book about sex. *The 80/80 Marriage* is about how to optimize your mindset and the structure of your life together to get the most out of marriage. And it just so happens that when you get more connected in life, you get more connected in the bedroom, in your most intimate moments.

It's also worth remembering that even for the most tightly connected 80/80 couples, sex can be extremely frustrating and complicated. Sexual energy is powerful. Its ways are unpredictable and it stirs up feelings that can be extremely intense.

All that is to say sex is so complex that this one chapter isn't going to give you everything you need to know. If you want to dive deeper into the world of sex and relationships, check out the resources on sex in the appendix. And if you or your partner are experiencing challenges in your intimate life that feel overwhelming and intractable, we strongly recommend seeking the help of a qualified professional.

Above all, it's worth remembering that encountering challenges in the bedroom doesn't mean you're doing anything wrong. It means you and your partner are like most other couples. You're both doing the best you can to figure out how to navigate the wildness and complexity of sexual desire.

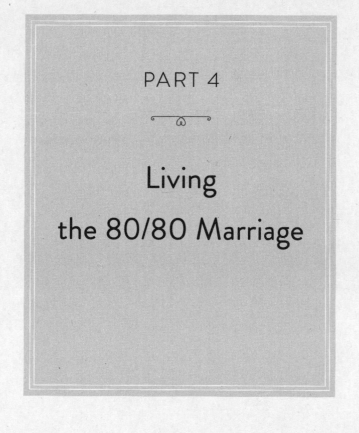

PART 4

Living
the 80/80 Marriage

CHAPTER 14

Resistance—The Reluctant Partner

*Note: You are about to read a chapter on what to do if you have a part-
ner who is reluctant to engage in the 80/80 model. The chapter assumes
you are in a relatively stable relationship, free from extreme forms of
coercion, barriers to exit, and emotional or physical abuse. If you're
experiencing any of these serious issues, the tools in this chapter are
unlikely to be helpful, and we suggest seeking professional help. If, on
the other hand, you find yourself in a stable relationship in which your
partner just happens to piss you off all the time by being unhelpful and
unengaged, this chapter was written just for you.*

Meet Josh and Melissa. Josh has one full-time job as a physician
assistant. Melissa has two jobs. She's a high school science teacher by
day and the family's full-time operations manager, cook, cleaning staff,
and event planner by night and by weekend.

Here's what a typical Saturday looks like for these two.

5:25 a.m.: Melissa hears their five-year-old daughter wandering into
their bedroom. "So much for sleeping in until seven," she
thinks. She gets up to read stories, leaving Josh sleeping.

6:30 a.m.: Melissa runs a load of laundry, plans out their meals for the
week, and comes up with a grocery list. Josh is still asleep.

7:40 a.m.: Melissa's now two hours into her Saturday. Josh gets up.

8 a.m.: Melissa has her one hour of free time for the day. She heads out to walk with a friend, while Josh shifts to what he calls "dad duty," making chocolate chip pancakes for the kids.

8:14 a.m.: Melissa's not even a mile into her walk when Josh texts: "Do we have another box of pancake batter?" and "Are we out of milk?" She interrupts her conversation to reply.

9 a.m.: Melissa returns to a mess of pancake batter spills and half-full cups of milk and orange juice. Josh leaves for the gym, while she cleans up the mess.

11:30 a.m.: Melissa takes her son to a soccer game, then drops off her daughter for a playdate. Josh watches college football and fires off a few emails during commercials.

2 p.m.: Melissa takes the kids to Target to buy them new clothes, then to the grocery store. Josh settles in for a nap on the couch.

4:30 p.m.: Even though she hates football, Melissa calls Josh's parents to help plan a Sunday afternoon Super Bowl party. Josh is still on the couch. He's now researching new golf clubs on the internet.

8:30 p.m.: Melissa spends forty-five minutes getting the kids ready for bed, helping them brush their teeth, and reading stories. Josh pulls the trigger on his big golf club purchase.

9:10 p.m.: Josh swoops in for a "super tuck-in" with the kids.

9:45 p.m.: Josh and Melissa lie together in bed. Josh is on his phone scanning social media and football scores on the ESPN app. Melissa is reading a book on marriage that she finds fascinating. She says to Josh, "I think some of the ideas in this book could be really helpful for us. If I flag some of the key parts for you, could we talk through this sometime?" Josh looks up momentarily from his iPhone and says, "Oh, babe, I would love to but I'm just so busy right now with work stuff."

Melissa replies, "OK," but deep down she feels a mixture of rage and exasperation. She thinks about saying something. But she doesn't want to have that fight again, not tonight. So she rolls over and goes to sleep.

The Reluctant Partner Problem

Josh is a textbook reluctant partner. He loves Melissa. He loves their life together. He's just not all that helpful, and he's also not that interested in books, practices, or conversations about making things better. That's Melissa's job.

Josh and millions of people like him are reluctant partners for two reasons. The first is that Josh and Melissa have settled into a classic dynamic of under- and over-contribution. As the under-contributing partner, Josh is reluctant to help in a significant way with childcare, cleaning, cooking, the social calendar, and the other logistics of daily life. But he is also a reluctant partner in another sense. Unlike Melissa, he's reluctant to engage fully in the mental and emotional project of making their marriage better.

The reluctant partner problem transcends traditional gender dynamics. While the statistics tell us that men are far more likely to be the reluctant partner, in some cases these roles are reversed, with women becoming the under-contributor. This dynamic can also arise in same-sex couples, with one partner over-contributing and the other becoming the under-contributing, more reluctant partner.

For some of you, the reluctant partner problem may be so deep and so difficult to solve that it could lead you to give up altogether on the idea of an 80/80 marriage. In fact, you may have even decided to skip ahead to read this chapter after just a few pages because of the gravity of this dilemma.

There are no easy solutions to this problem. But it's one worth trying to solve. When the resistance and reluctance of the under-contributing partner fall away, living the 80/80 marriage becomes easier. Radical generosity can become a common mindset. Shared success can become a common goal. In short, overcoming this obstacle is often the key to spending less time arguing about fairness and more time working together as an 80/80 team.

Why It's No Fun

At the risk of stating the obvious, having a reluctant partner is no fun. You feel the constant burden of having to manage everything. You feel unappreciated for all the things you do. Each day, you wake up to a background hum of resentment that never quite goes away, even in your best moments together. The whole experience can leave you feeling overwhelmed, irritated, and totally exhausted.

And yet it's not necessarily fun to be the reluctant partner either. Take Chris. The strain of the reluctant partner dynamic resulted in his marriage falling apart and ending in divorce. In this relationship, Chris was the reluctant partner. And while it might sound like the perfect arrangement to have your partner do everything, being on the reluctant partner side of this dynamic comes with its own flavor of emotional suffering. As he told us, "There was a scorecard in my marriage. The dynamic that played out was that my wife wanted to do everything. So I stopped doing anything, which isn't my nature. I'm usually a doer. And then the story in our marriage became, 'Chris doesn't do anything.' So I just shut down and became resentful because my contribution was expected. It wasn't a gift to the marriage. It was me taking orders."

What we learn from Chris is that the reluctant partner problem isn't just a problem for the over-contributor. It's a painful dynamic that leads to suffering on both sides.

Who's to Blame?

Like sex, all sorts of complicated cultural and gender dynamics influence the way we perceive the reluctant partner problem. In heterosexual marriages, when the wife over-contributes and the husband is the reluctant partner, we're often told that men are to blame.

As we have seen throughout the book, male-dominated power structures have irrevocably shaped the state of modern relationships. The antiquated 80/20 model of men working at the office and women toiling away at home continues to influence the experience of modern marriage. Even in households with progressive beliefs about gender equality or those in which the woman out earns the man, this historical hangover creates a silent momentum that often results in a reluctant (male) partner.

This cultural backdrop of inequality coupled with the statistical fact that men do less has led many feminist scholars to give up on the very idea of marriage. As Gloria Steinem, the early pioneer of feminism, asserts, what's the point of getting hitched when "marriage makes you legally a half person"?[1] What's more, she says, "marriage has worked out better for men than for women. The two happiest groups are married men and unmarried women."[2]

There's now an entire genre of marriage books, articles, and podcasts out there lamenting all the ways men have created the reluctant partner problem. As feminist author Jessica Valenti puts it, "It's not actually motherhood or kids that derail women's careers and personal ambitions—it's men who refuse to do their fair share." She goes on to say, "It's not that women can't 'have it all,' it's that men won't stop taking it."[3]

There is a lot of truth to this narrative. It's true that women most often find themselves in the role of over-contributor. It's true that men tend to slip into the role of doing less and becoming a reluctant partner. It's true that age-old structures of gender inequality continue to influence these dynamics.

And yet all of this glosses over something important: the complicated truth that in the actual practice of a marriage, both partners play a role in creating this dynamic. By focusing solely on the bad actions of reluctant partners or, in this case, men, the over-contributing partner can become disempowered. They may resent their reluctant partner. They may complain to friends about the injustice of the situation. But they may also forget to ask two essential questions: "Can we change this dynamic?" and "Are there ways I have contributed to having a reluctant partner?"

These are the questions we will be exploring in the rest of this chapter. They are questions that can be uncomfortable to ask. They may push against your ordinary assumptions of who's to blame. But just for now, we encourage you to step outside the comfort zone of seeing the reluctant partner as the problem.

Of course, this doesn't mean you should now see yourself as the problem. It means seeing the larger dynamic, which you both play a role in creating, as the problem. It means shifting the conversation from the question of "Who's to blame?" to a more helpful question: "How can we break this pattern that is making us both miserable?"

It's a radical experiment. It takes courage and an open mind. But it also just might change your life.

The Subtle Benefits of Doing It All

So how might you—the one who's doing everything—be contributing to the reluctant partner dynamic? Consider Tina. She is a classic over-contributing spouse. We interviewed her by phone while she was parked in the garage with her eighteen-month-old child sleeping in the back seat. This thirty-minute nap window, she told us, was her only "free time" to talk all day.

Tina used the analogy of buckets to help paint the picture of what it's like to be married to a reluctant partner. "I've got multiple buckets," she said. "I've got my work bucket, and I've got my friend bucket, and I've got multiple kids buckets, and I've got the paying-the-bills bucket. And my husband—God love him—he only has one or two buckets."

We asked Tina what was keeping her husband from taking on more buckets.

"I have no idea," she said. "Maybe it's just that we naturally fall into these traditional roles. But maybe part of the problem is that I become complacent. Sometimes, I'll complain about how I do everything, but I also sometimes think about how I really like to have more control over everything."

As she reflected further, she came to an even deeper insight. She explained to us that in some ways, she's actually contributing to a setup in which she does it all and her husband does almost nothing. "Even though I'm a mess, and I can barely keep up with it all, there's something comforting about knowing that I have my hand in every bucket in our life. I always know what's going on, and I know that I could do it all on my own if I needed to. My husband, on the other hand, has no clue what's going on. He asks me eighteen times each week what time the soccer game is happening on Saturday."

Tina revealed two profound insights during our conversation. The first is that, like many over-contributing partners, she may be contributing to this dynamic by being complacent and not asking for what she really wants. The second is that some part of her doesn't actually want to change the pattern because there are benefits to doing it all. This is a wild insight that takes a lot of self-awareness to see. And yet seeing that you may contribute and even benefit from this pattern is often the first step to overcoming the reluctant partner problem.

Shifting the Reluctant Partner Pattern

So how can you break out of the reluctant partner pattern? In an ideal world, this two-person problem would come with a two-person solution. The two of you, together, created this dynamic. If you're the over-contributing partner, you created it by avoiding making sincere requests for help or clinging to the sense of control that comes with doing everything. If you're the reluctant partner, you created it by missing opportunities to be helpful or acting out on the worst of your passive-aggressive instincts.

The problem, however, is that we don't live in an ideal world. By definition, reluctant partners may not ever take the initiative to change this dynamic. They are, after all, reluctant. This means that change may unfortunately have to start with you, the partner who is doing it all. We realize the extreme injustice of this. It's like saying, "Even though you're the one who already does everything, you're the one who should also make the first move in breaking this pattern." It's outrageously unfair.

But even though it might not be fair, looking at how you (the over-contributing partner) can address this problem might be the best thing you can do for yourself and for the health of your marriage. Your courageous and radically generous actions might, in the end, be the only way to shift the pattern.

What does it look like for an over-contributing partner to begin breaking the pattern in real time? To see how it might be possible, let's revisit Melissa and Josh. When we look more closely at Melissa's day, we find all sorts of hidden opportunities for her to push Josh to become more involved, to become engaged, and, let's face it, to act less like a twenty-year-old living in a fraternity house and more like a grown-up. These changes are subtle. But they can lead to profound shifts in the reluctant partner dynamic.

When Josh texts her at 8:14 a.m., does Melissa *have* to interrupt her walk to text back the location of the pancake mix? Or could she turn off her phone, enjoy the walk, and trust that her husband will figure out a way for the kids to eat? When she returns home, what would happen if she said to Josh, "Looks like you guys had a great time. Can you please grab the kids and clean all this up while I take a shower?"

During the afternoon, what would happen if she asked Josh to take their younger daughter to her playdate and swing by the grocery store on the way back? Sure, he might buy the wrong kind of ketchup or forget to purchase organic strawberries. But that might be a small price to pay for a more open afternoon.

In the late afternoon, perhaps she could just *not* make the call about the Super Bowl party. If it's really important to Josh, maybe he'll set it up. If he doesn't, that's great too. She no longer has to go to a party she's dreading.

And at the end of the day, when Melissa asks Josh to read the book she's interested in, why let him off the hook with a simple OK? What would happen if she revealed her frustration, saying, "Having this conversation about improving our marriage is important to me. I really want you to read the pages I flagged sometime next week so that next Saturday night we can have this conversation."

The point here is that some over-contributing partners, like Melissa, aren't asking for what they really want, aren't revealing the hard truths, and aren't willing to push back in a spirit of radical generosity against the failure of their reluctant partner to become more engaged in the relationship.

Can You Really Engage a Reluctant Partner?

The idea of unwinding this dynamic by changing your behavior as an over-contributing partner might still sound absurd. You might still wonder if this is some sort of marital pipe dream we're peddling—a grand-sounding idea that's never actually worked in real life.

We understand the skepticism, and that when you're locked into a pattern like this, breaking out of it can seem impossible. But we also know that this shift *is* possible because after spending years stuck in this dynamic, we finally found a way out.

Here's how it played out for us. When we got married at the age of twenty-six, Kaley was a high-functioning adult. She organized everything neatly into spreadsheets and folders. She reconciled her finances each month. She thought carefully about retirement planning, regularly did laundry, and had an IRA. Nate, by contrast, lived like he was still in college. He didn't really track his spending. He was on a biannual cleaning schedule for his apartment. And as a grad student in political philosophy, the only IRA he had ever heard of was a militant political group in Ireland.

When we started living together, our two worlds collided. Kaley naturally stepped into the role of handling everything. Nate learned that he could basically just kick back and never really worry about boring logistics like renewing auto insurance or paying a cell phone bill. Nor did he have to worry about exploring ways to grow closer as a couple. Kaley had him covered. And that's how we lived for years.

This pattern was painful for Kaley. She felt like she carried all the weight of the marriage on her shoulders. She also felt constant resentment toward Nate. Each time he dropped a ball, failed to follow through, or didn't acknowledge how hard she was working, she felt annoyed and upset.

From the outside, it might seem like Nate had the perfect setup. But this pattern didn't work out well for him either. Each time Kaley delegated a trip to the store or reminded him to get the sprinklers fixed, he also got irritated and upset. He felt like no matter what he did, it was never enough. So at a certain point, he concluded, "If I can never do enough, I might as well stop trying so hard."

How did the pattern finally shift? Kaley started asking herself the same questions we asked about Melissa's day. Questions like:

- What if I just stopped unloading the dishwasher right away and asked for help?
- What if I revealed my frustration in a mature way every time Nate said he would do something but didn't follow through?
- What would happen if I handed some of the big tasks on my plate—like all our finances—over to Nate?

- What if I told Nate that going to a relationship seminar together was really important to me?

Take the finances question. For years, Kaley resented Nate because she spent hours paying the credit card bill, tracking monthly expenses, budgeting, and filing taxes. And yet when she was honest with herself, she also realized she didn't want Nate to take over finances. Why? Because she didn't want to lose control. This insight helped her to see that to get a more engaged husband and joy for herself, she had to be willing to give up control in some areas.

So one day, five years in, she asked Nate to take over our finances. Nate said yes, and after hours of explanation that gave him a true appreciation for all she had been doing, Kaley never had to pay another credit card or electric bill again. Nate was reluctant at first, but soon he grew more interested in our family finances, building out new systems and spreadsheets. It's a transformation that took time. But it all started with a single hard conversation and Kaley's willingness to let go of control.

The same thing happened with Nate's early aversion to working on our marriage. Instead of telling herself the story that he just wasn't that interested, Kaley told Nate, "It's important to me that you come with me to this weekend seminar." Nate went. He was reluctant but open to learn. And then something unexpected happened. He found the seminar so interesting that he started reading books on relationships and self-improvement. And now, fifteen years later, this work has become our shared passion. It never would have happened without that initial hard conversation.

The point here is that our pattern shifted only because Kaley was willing to ask for what she wanted, and though Nate was reluctant, he was curious enough to try something new. Take away either of these conditions—Kaley's push or Nate's reluctant curiosity—and we would still be stuck.

There's one other subtlety worth mentioning. It's an insight we weren't aware of until years after the fact. Nate took Kaley's requests seriously because on some deep level, he knew that she was willing to leave. She never said it. She never threatened it. But she knew and Nate knew that the status quo pattern of Nate as the under-contributing partner wasn't a long-term option she would tolerate. And that subtle knowing further motivated Nate to change.

Some Partners Aren't Just Reluctant, They're Unwilling

Our story raises a critical question: What happens if the engaged partner addresses all the ways they've contributed to having an unengaged spouse but the reluctant partner remains totally unwilling to change? At that point, the problem shifts. You're no longer dealing with a reluctant partner. You're dealing with an unwilling partner.

The shift sounds subtle, but unwillingness in marriage is a world apart from reluctance. Reluctant partners may have some hesitation, but they're open to change. Unwilling partners, by contrast, have barricaded the path to change. They're unwilling to try anything new, to take on more of the load, to respond to a sincere request, or to engage in the project of growing as a couple. It's expressed with a clear, "I'm not doing that."

If you're dealing with a reluctant partner, the tools in this chapter can help you shift closer to the 80/80 model. If you're dealing with an unwilling partner, however, you might need more than this book to bring about a transformation in your relationship.

When your partner is completely unwilling to change or even to seek help through marriage counseling, you're often left with a heartbreaking choice between two unfortunate options. One of these options is to consider leaving the relationship, a life-altering choice that brings with it extreme emotional and logistical chaos. The other option is to make the best of a bad situation—to do your best to accept the fact that your partner is unwilling.

These are both difficult options. And yet whichever path you choose, the tools of the 80/80 model can still be useful to you. If you choose to leave your marriage, radical generosity can help you manage the emotional turmoil that follows in the wake of divorce. If you choose to stay, shifting your mindset to radical generosity can change *your* experience of marriage. If you cook every meal for the kids with a mindset of fairness, for instance, you're guaranteed to feel resentment at the end of each meal. If, however, you shift to radical generosity, you can at least begin the process of letting go of these negative emotions. You can, at the very least, know that you are doing the best you can in the midst of a challenging situation.

Letting Go of Doing Everything

Assuming you're dealing with a reluctant rather than an unwilling partner, here's a simple thought experiment, designed to help you move toward a specific plan for dissolving this dynamic. The experiment comes from Gay and Katie Hendricks, two of the world's leading experts on relationships and conscious living. They wrote something that just about knocked us out of our chairs the first time we read it: "In all times and every way, we are getting exactly what we're committed to getting."[4]

Take a moment to let that sink in.

If you're like us, your initial reaction might be resistance and defensiveness. Your mind might flood with thoughts like "That can't possibly be true!" or "You've never met my spouse!" or "How could I possibly be committed to a life where I do everything? That's insane!"

But just for a moment, just for right now, imagine that's true. Imagine you're committed to getting exactly what you're getting in your marriage. Imagine you're the one writing the script of the play of life in which your partner doesn't contribute and doesn't care about improving the marriage. Imagine that you are 100 percent responsible for your partner's reluctance to engage.

It's a crazy idea. But it's also an idea that just might change your marriage forever. It's the idea you'll explore even more deeply in the following practice.

How Am I Committed to This?

80/80 PRACTICE

This practice requires you to take a giant leap—to imagine a world where you are committed to your partner's reluctance. Whether that's true or not isn't important. What's important is that you go all in with this thought experiment to see what new insights this radical perspective brings.

Step 1: Own your commitment

The first step is to get really curious. It's as simple as saying to yourself in the privacy of your own mind: *Somehow, I am committed to having a reluctant and unengaged partner.*

Step 2: The training manual

Now it's time to unpack that "somehow" in the line above—to explore how exactly you're committed to having a reluctant and unengaged partner. Here's how to do it. Imagine your task is to create a training manual with specific action steps for others. But this isn't a normal training manual. It's not about what to do. It's more about what *not* to do. This is a training manual titled "How to Have a Reluctant and Unengaged Partner, Just Like Me." It's your chance to instruct others on how to create a relationship in which they end up doing everything and having a reluctant and unengaged partner. Here's an example:

Tip 1: Do all the dishes without ever asking for help. Then lash out at your partner because they're "not helpful."

Tip 2:   Ask for help on something—just once. When your partner doesn't immediately jump in with a great attitude, use it as proof that they suck, and don't ever ask again.

Tip 3:   When your partner texts you, "Can you pick up my guitar from the shop on your way back from work?" say, "Sure," even though you don't have time. Then resent them for it.

Tip 4:   When you feel like you handle 95 percent of the housework, don't ever have a conversation about adjusting your roles. Just complain about it with your friends.

Tip 5:   If you feel inspired to try out some new strategies to improve your marriage, it's best to just assume your partner would never be open to it. Then feel angry at them for being so withdrawn and uninterested.

Now it's your turn. Write out your training manual tips below.

Tip 1: _____

_____

Tip 2: _____

_____

Tip 3: _____

_____

Tip 4: _____

_____

Tip 5: _____

_____

Tip 6: _____

_____

Step 3: The costs and benefits of your commitment

It may sound strange, but with patterns like this, there is always both a cost and a benefit. For example, never asking for help might cost you having an engaged partner, but the benefit, as we saw earlier, is that you get visibility into everything that's happening in life and you get near-total control. What are the costs and benefits of your version of this pattern?

WHAT'S THE COST?	WHAT'S THE BENEFIT?
Examples: • I rarely get a good night's sleep. • I'm always angry and resentful.	Examples: • I get to be a "superwoman" who does it all. • I get to avoid having hard conversations.

Step 4: Making a new commitment

If you've stayed with us this far, you're now starting to see both how you're committed to having a reluctant partner as well as what this pattern costs you. At this point you may say, "the benefits outweigh the costs." You may, in other words, decide to consciously accept having a reluctant partner. This is actually a gift because it allows you to continue in your relationship without as much resentment because you have chosen this arrangement. You have made it a conscious choice.

If, however, you want to change your commitment, we encourage you to think of a few actions you could take to shift to a new commitment, one that sounds more like "I am committed to having a helpful and engaged partner." For this to work, these action steps should be real options within your control. For example:

Action 1:   I am going to ask my partner to do the Roles for Shared Success practice on page 109 with me.

Action 2:   I am going to leave my partner's texts unanswered for an hour when they make outrageous requests.

Action 3:   I am going to talk to my partner about taking one long weekend away from the family every year for a getaway with my friends or a restorative retreat.

Now it's your turn:

Action 1: _____

Action 2: _____

Action 3: _____

Action 4: _____

Action 5: _____

Tip 1: RG

Be radically generous with yourself—this isn't easy.

Tip 2: What? RG again?

Be radically generous with your partner. He or she will mirror your mindset. If you go on the attack, your partner will almost certainly fire back. If you approach them with radical generosity, though, they might at first wonder, "What the hell is happening?" But then they just might soften their tone and respond to these actions in ways you never could have expected.

CHAPTER 15

Rituals—The 5 Essential Habits of the 80/80 Marriage

At the risk of pointing out the obvious, you are now in the final pages of *The 80/80 Marriage*. We think it's worth noting because you're getting close to putting down this book, perhaps forever. And that leaves you with an important choice between two very different ways of bringing the 80/80 model into your life.

One way is to see this model as a bunch of ideas, some of which could be helpful to you and your partner. The other way is to see it as a practice, as a moment-to-moment way of being in marriage. This more practical view is less about ideas and more about habits. Instead of thinking about the power of radical generosity, it's turning generosity into your ordinary mindset. Instead of talking about the idea of shared success, it's building new structures in your life around the question "What's best for us?"

If your goal is to experience real change—to grow and deepen your connection with your partner—then the choice is clear. The 80/80 model can't just be an idea. It has to become a practice.

Why? Because big life changes rarely come from an idea, concept, conversation, or book alone. They come when ideas turn into ordinary and automatic habits, woven deep into the fabric of ordinary life.

You have no doubt experienced this yourself. You read a book that blows your mind. It opens you up to new ways of thinking. For a week or two, the insights feel fresh and alive. You wake up thinking about these new life-changing ideas. You bring up the ideas at coffee with a friend, during a quick conversation with a coworker, or when you're lying in bed late at night with your partner.

But soon, this game-changing book moves from your nightstand to a basement shelf. It's no longer the topic of conversation with your partner or your friends. In just a matter of weeks, what was once a source of inspiration has all but disappeared from your life.

That's the way it goes with most inspiring new books, ideas, podcasts, or weekend retreats. We say all this to highlight an essential fact: *Ideas and insights quickly fade. But habits and practices tend to stick around.*

A Marriage of Habit

While it's easy to think it's the big moments that define our experience of marriage—the weeklong trip to Costa Rica or that romantic Valentine's Day dinner at an expensive restaurant—it's really the other 99 percent of life's moments, the ones shaped by microscopic habits, that create the atmosphere of our life together.

Our entire day is made up of these microscopic moments.

These habits can be things like giving your partner a hug when they return from work—*good habit*. Bragging about your partner's latest win at work in front of friends—*good habit*. Leaning over to your partner in bed before you fall asleep each night to offer a kiss and say, "I love you"—*another good habit*.

Or they can be things like only half listening to your partner because you're too busy reading product reviews about a new electric toothbrush on Amazon—*bad habit*. Feeling pissed off at something your partner said but deciding it's not worth the effort to reveal the issue—*bad habit*.

Or keeping a detailed mental log of all the amazing things you've done so you can finally build a knockdown argument to prove, once and for all, that things aren't perfectly fair in your house—*a really bad habit.*

While they may sound small and subtle, these habits have enormous power, which springs from the invisible and subconscious nature of these acts. Habits are by their very definition easy, automatic, and effortless.[1] We don't have to think about them. They just kind of happen.

And that's why our habits outlast even the most life-altering epiphanies. Long after inspiration fades, our habits live on in the background, silently directing the show of marriage and life.

The Habit of 80/80

If marriage is just a collection of habits, then how can we change them? How can we reinforce the good ones and replace the bad ones? One of the best answers comes from what author Charles Duhigg calls the *loop of habit.*[2] To understand this loop, consider smartphone addiction, that nasty little habit that leaves us staring into our screens at dinner, while attempting to play with our children at the park, or even while driving seventy miles per hour down a busy interstate.

Here's the loop. It all starts with a *cue,* a trigger that initiates the action. In this case, the cue might be that *ding* of your smartphone alerting you to a new text or news update. Or in other cases, the cue might be in your own mind—that uncomfortable feeling of being bored while sitting in a doctor's office waiting room that compels you to lose yourself in Facebook, your email, or breaking news.

This cue leads to a *routine,* the action you take in response to the cue. In this case, the routine is checking Facebook, scanning your inbox, or scrolling through the latest news.

The routine sets up the final part of the loop of habit, the part that hooks us, keeping us coming back again and again for more: the *reward.* The reward you get from your smartphone is that brief dopamine-induced hit of pleasure that strikes the moment the mystery surrounding what's in your in-box or News Feed is revealed to you.[3]

This loop shows how our current habits have hooked us. But it also shows how we can make new habits that lead us toward, instead of away from, connection, love, and intimacy. To turn the ideas of the 80/80 model—ideas such as radical generosity and shared success—into habits, we need to create a similar loop. We need a cue, a clear and simple routine, and a reward.

The cue is like an alarm clock, waking us up from unhelpful ways of relating to our partner. A cue makes us aware of the possibility of doing something different, of shifting from fairness to radical generosity, or from what's best for me to what's best for us.

The routine is a specific action we can take to create change. It's actually writing that love note and putting it on your partner's desk. It's revealing that issue with your partner that's been hijacking your attention for hours, and making a reasonable request. It's making that big decision on the basis of what's best for us.

The reward happens naturally. You don't need to manufacture it by buying yourself a latte or doing a touchdown dance in the hallway. You just need to notice the experience of connection that inevitably results from the habits of the 80/80 model and savor that feeling. When you write a love note, for example, the reward is that instantaneous feeling that comes from a generous act. When you reveal that issue, the reward is the experience of closeness. When you make a decision based on your values of shared success, the reward is feeling the power struggle fade away.

This is the formula for building new 80/80 habits. For each of the habits outlined below, we will prompt you to think of:

- A specific way to implement the 80/80 routine
- The frequency with which you intend to carry out this new routine (once a day, once a week, once a year, etc.)
- A cue to trigger the habit

We haven't listed the reward because it's the same for all these habits: that amazing shift in mood, energy, and spirit that happens when you feel more connected. When this shift happens, notice it, savor it, and let yourself settle into this raw experience of love.[4]

The Five Essential Habits of 80/80

Over the course of this book, we've thrown all sorts of practices at you. We've explored practices to cultivate a mindset of radical generosity: contribution, appreciation, and revealing. We've also explored practices to build a structure of shared success: roles, priorities, boundaries, power, and sex. All these practices can be turned into habits.

And yet we also want to leave you with a curated list of the five most powerful habits of the 80/80 model. In our lives and the lives of the people we interviewed, we noticed the same five habits come up again and again. These habits offer a rapid pathway to connection, love, and intimacy. Some of them relate directly to the 80/80 model; others are more about creating the ideal conditions for it to thrive.

To experience the full benefits of the 80/80 model, we strongly recommend turning at least the first three of these into regular habits. If you can add all five over time, you'll experience an even deeper transformation.

That said, you don't have to add all these habits at once. Because building habits requires discipline and will, we recommend taking a gradual approach, building one at a time. And, of course, you may decide that some of the other practices in the book not listed here would offer you and your partner the most value. That's perfectly fine. Trust your intuition in terms of where to invest your time and energy.

Habit 1: Create Space for Connection

If we had to distill the modern predicament of marriage down to two words, they would be: *no space.*

Couples from all walks of life told us this is the number one challenge they face. As one father of triplets living in Manhattan put it, "We get so wrapped up in the kids' needs, school, and food that we become husband-and-wife servants for the kids; we can easily forget about each other, how we met, and why we want to be together." Another woman we interviewed observed, "There's no room for connection. There's just a whole lot of doing."

So how can we create space in marriage for connection? Thriving couples rely on three primary types of habits: micro, medium, and macro habits.

Micro habits are the subtle ways we stay connected in the midst of even the most chaotic days. It's taking the dog out for a ten-minute walk together after dinner. It's greeting each other with a kiss and a long hug. It's having a family dinner. It's talking through your day while lying in bed. It's sharing your appreciation at meals. It's doing a quick emotional check-in by asking: "How are you *really* doing?" The happiest couples we spoke with used these micro habits to stay connected in the midst of life.

Medium habits require carving out space on the calendar. Date night was the medium habit shared most frequently by the couples we interviewed. Others, however, had their own clever alternatives to going out to dinner on a Friday night. They talked about "ditch days," in which they cut out of work together for a couple of hours to watch a movie. "Adult swim time," in which they went skinny-dipping for thirty minutes during the workday. Or, our personal favorite, the "date hike," which we do religiously every Saturday morning, rain, shine, sleet, or snow.

Macro habits require going away to spend long stretches of time together. Some couples talked about yearly vacations alone together, without the kids. Others could only fit in a weekend once a year. Venture investor Brad Feld and his wife, Amy Batchelor, told us about their ritual of "Qx vacations," in which the Q stands for *quarterly* and the *x* stands for whether it's the first, second, third, or fourth quarter of the year, which is the frequency of these "off-the-grid" trips for connection.[5] You may not be able to take a quarterly trip. But even a day or two a year when you have the time and space together to connect can have a huge impact on the health of your marriage.

To turn creating space for connection into a regular practice, come up with some of your own ideas for habits in each of these three areas.

Creating Space for Connection

80/80 PRACTICE

What micro, medium, and macro habits can you use to create more space for connection? Use the chart below to think through the specific rituals, frequency, and cues you might use to carve out space for greater intimacy and connection.

	RITUAL	FREQUENCY	CUE
MICRO HABITS	*Example:* Walking the dog together	*Example:* Once a day	*Example:* When we see each other after work
MEDIUM HABITS	*Example:* Date night, date hike, ditch day	*Example:* Once a week	*Example:* Wednesday nights
MACRO HABITS	*Example:* A road trip, a couples retreat	*Example:* Twice a year	*Example:* The first week of July, Labor Day

Habit 2: The Call-and-Response of Radical Generosity

As with any habit, it's easy to talk about all the amazing benefits of the 80/80 mindset of radical generosity. Actually living in this mindset, on the other hand, is often difficult. It requires constant remembering and daily practice, especially when life gets crazy.

To spend more time living in this mindset, we recommend initiating the call-and-response of contribution and appreciation once a day. This involves two interconnected daily habits.

The first is doing one radically generous act a day. This is your chance to express radical generosity through contribution—a hug, a card, a clean kitchen floor, or a fresh cup of coffee delivered to your partner in bed. It's an act that has the power to break through the fog of resentment and trigger an upward spiral of generosity between you and your partner.

The second habit is about what you see. It's paying close attention to your partner's acts of contribution throughout the day and then appreciating them for their work. It's telling them, "You look amazing today in that new shirt," "I saw you out there pulling weeds in the lawn. Thanks for your work on that," or "I've been noticing how much time you're spending with our son, tutoring him in math. I really appreciate all the work you're doing to help him."

One of these radically generous acts often leads to two or three or ten, which is how these daily habits can slowly transform all areas of your life.

Daily Contribution and Appreciation   80/80 PRACTICE

Now it's your chance to think about how you want to build the habit of contribution and appreciation. As you fill this out, you'll notice one essential difference between these two concepts. contribution works best when the ritual varies from day to day—it might be making a meal one day, writing a note the next, or cleaning the kitchen floor the day after. Appreciation, by contrast, is simpler. It involves the same ritual each day—expressing one thing you appreciate about your partner. All this is to say that it can be helpful to write out a variety of rituals under contribution, but there's no need to do the same for appreciation.

	RITUAL	FREQUENCY	CUE
CONTRIBUTION	*Example:* Making coffee, unloading the dishwasher, leaving a love note	*Example:* Once a day	*Example:* Waking up or when planning out my week
APPRECIATION	*Example:* One genuine expression of appreciation	*Example:* Once a day	*Example:* During dinner or before falling asleep

Habit 3: Reveal Issues, Misunderstandings, and Resentments as They Arise

Imagine your partner just insulted you in front of friends at a dinner party. Imagine they forgot to pick up your child from camp, leaving Junior waiting outside in the rain for more than an hour. Imagine they were forty-five minutes late to your Thursday date night but didn't call or text to let you know. These are problems.

But these issues get much worse when you don't reveal your true experience and instead spend days or even weeks stewing in passive-aggressiveness or lashing out at your partner over meaningless stuff, all because you don't want to have a direct conversation and face the issue head-on.

That's why one of the most essential habits of the 80/80 model is to reveal issues as they arise. As we discussed in chapter seven, you don't have to go through an elaborate process. All you have to do is Reveal and Request: reveal your experience and make a reasonable request.

This is the habit of hearing the insult at the dinner party and then telling your partner afterward, "When you made that joke at dinner, it really hurt my feelings. Please be more careful about what you say next time." It's telling your partner after the forgotten pickup at camp, "I feel scared when you forget to pick up our child. I feel like I can't trust you. Can you please set an alarm next time?" Or it's telling them when they arrive forty-five minutes late, "When you show up late without texting me, it makes me feel like you value your time over mine. Can you please make a point of letting me know when you're running late?"

You're not just doing yourself a favor by revealing the issue so you can get back in sync with your partner. You're also doing your partner a favor by giving them important feedback on how to be a better husband, wife, lover, friend, and logistics partner.

Reveal Issues as They Arise

80/80
PRACTICE

Reveal and Request is a situational habit. It's something you do when you feel triggered, irritated, or resentful. So the best cue is your emotional state. When you feel out of sync, upset, hurt, or angry toward your partner, that's a sign that it's a good time to express a Reveal and Request.

	RITUAL	FREQUENCY	CUE
REVEAL AND REQUEST	*Example:* Expressing a Reveal and Request	*Example:* When issues arise or at the end of each day	*Example:* Feeling resentment, anger, or sadness toward my partner

Habit 4: The Shared-Success Check-in

There's a bit of controversy surrounding what's become known as the "family meeting," that time when couples sit together like co-CEOs in the boardroom, hammering out plans, goals, and logistics.

On one side, you have the couples who swear by it. Consider Tim and Heather. As they told us, "Having partner meetings, or 'tagging up,' as we call it, is our forced time to pause and look at the schedule, see what's going on for the week, and see the bigger picture. When we don't do it, things become explosively bad." Or, as another woman revealed to us, "If we don't set aside time to meet together, then date night becomes all about logistics, which is so not romantic."

Other couples, however, resist the corporate formality of having meetings. They see these check-ins as not at all sexy and a bit contrived.

We understand the aversion to turning your marriage into a business strategy session. But here's the problem. At a certain point, sharing a life starts to get really complicated. You start with the responsibility-free experience of dating. Then you add one or two demanding careers. You add sharing space. You add a house or apartment. You add kids. You add a few unexpected health issues. You add aging parents. You add a global pandemic to the mix. And suddenly, running a household together becomes about as demanding as managing any other complex enterprise.

You can ignore this fact, wishing things could magically go back to the freewheeling early days, when your biggest problem was figuring out whose turn it was to pay for groceries—a bad choice. Or you can revert to an 80/20 model, in which one partner does it all—an even worse choice. Or you can accept the reality that modern marriage involves an overwhelming amount of logistical complexity and begin to build structures to handle the logistics of life more skillfully—the choice we recommend.

You can do this by building the habit of a shared-success family check-in. This is a time dedicated to staying in sync about the logistics of life. It could be a short conversation at the beginning of each day. It could be a longer check-in once a week. It could even be an extended time for reflection a few times a year, in which you take a step back and look at the big picture.

Here's one pro tip for making the most of these check-ins: make a point of seeing if you can stay in the spirit of radical generosity and shared success. Notice when you get hooked by the tendency to think about what's best for you. Then remember to shift back to the essential question of 80/80 shared success: "What's best for us?"

Shared-Success Check-ins

80/80 PRACTICE

We recommend two types of shared-success check-ins. The first are those regular (daily or weekly) check-ins that help you stay on top of the logistics of life. The second are the occasional longer check-ins that allow you to take a step back and explore larger structural changes in roles, priorities, boundaries, power, or sex.

	RITUAL	FREQUENCY	CUE
SHORT CHECK-INS	*Example:* Looking at calendars together	*Example:* Once a day or once a week	*Example:* When we wake up on Sunday morning
BIG-PICTURE CHECK-INS	*Example:* Looking together through roles, priorities, boundaries, power, and sex	*Example:* Every three months or once a year	*Example:* At the beginning of each year

Habit 5: Create Space from Digital Distractions

During the writing of this book, we heard some tragic stories of affairs, divorce, and intractable conflicts. And yet some of the most tragic stories involved a subtler form of disconnection. They were the stories of two partners sitting in bed each night, staring into the screens of their smartphones and tablets, so entranced by Twitter, blogs, news sites, or games that the other person all but disappeared. They were the stories of one partner trying to have an important conversation, talk through plans, or reveal an issue but feeling like the other person was "not all there," half paying attention to the conversation, half paying attention to the device in their hand.

These stories point to a larger cultural experience. On some level, we're all living in what psychologist Linda Stone has called a state of *continuous partial attention*, never fully on, never fully off, always slightly distracted from what's happening in the present moment.[6]

In marriage, this shows up as yet another barrier to connection. The seductive draw of the device in our pocket distracts us from our desire for real seduction—the good kind, the kind that thrusts us back into being fully present, together. Put bluntly, many of us are having an emotional affair with our email, texts, social media, the news, or games. And it's an affair that's standing in the way of a more fulfilling marriage.

There's a simple but not always easy way to put an end to this pattern: create time and space away from digital distraction. The couples we interviewed talked about all kinds of ways to do this:

- Keep smartphones and tablets out of the bedroom.
- Lock devices in a box during focused time, like at the dinner table.
- Establish a norm of asking each other permission each time you use your phone in the other's presence by saying, "Is now a good time for me to respond to this text?"
- If it's possible, go for a walk or go out for an entire date night and leave both of your phones behind.
- Use "Do Not Disturb" mode to screen out random calls and texts during couple time.
- Never have sex with a phone nearby.
- Before looking something up or checking your phone, ask yourself, "Do I really need to know this, right now?" You may be surprised to find that the answer is generally no.

Creating Space from Digital Distractions 80/80 PRACTICE

Consider how you and your partner get hooked by digital distraction. Then come up with one to three rituals to create space in your life where you can be more connected and focused on the things that really matter.

	RITUAL	FREQUENCY	CUE
CREATING SPACE FROM DIGITAL DISTRACTIONS	*Example:* Keeping devices out of sight	*Example:* Every day	*Example:* When we're in bed

The more all five of these habits become a regular, almost automatic part of your life together, the greater connection, intimacy, and joy you will experience.

Refresh Your Practice of the 80/80 Marriage

Want to go deeper? We've found that a few hours together or, occasionally, a full day together reviewing these practices is one of the best ways to supercharge these habits. During the writing of this book, many of the couples we spoke with agreed. In fact, they started asking us for exercises and tips on how to create their own self-guided marriage check-ins, date nights, and couples retreats.

Inspired by these requests, we have developed a number of resources to help you continue to grow your practice of the 80/80 marriage over time. These resources include daily insights and challenges, PDF downloads on a wide range of marriage topics, and even a series of 80/80 self-guided virtual retreats that you can do with your partner anytime, anywhere. For more information, visit our website: www.8080Marriage.com.

EPILOGUE

There's a reason modern marriage often seems confusing, contradictory, and even impossible. It's a tension that we've kept bumping up against, both throughout the fifteen years of our marriage and while interviewing other couples in the process of writing this book. Put simply, it's the tension between two conflicting aims that shape our life: our desire to shine as individuals and our desire to share a life with another.

The first of these has been hammered deep into our subconscious by a culture that celebrates unbridled individualism. We're told from early on to dream big, to do great things, and to change the world. We worship at the feet of exceptional individuals: rock stars, thought leaders, celebrities, Instagram influencers, and business leaders. To succeed in life, we are told, we must be *somebody*, do something amazing, be the best self we can be.

But then along comes marriage, this old-school relic of the past designed to be anything but individualistic. In fact, it's the opposite. Marriage and long-term relationships call on us to merge, to unify our separate plans, goals, and ambitions.

And we wonder why relationships are so hard. We wonder why so many successful and intelligent people fail to make it work. We wonder why so many marriages that look healthy from the outside end in divorce.

Marriage and relationships force us to do an instant cultural 180, to suddenly become part of a greater whole, right at the moment when we're beginning to hit our stride as individuals. Moments after we say, "I do," we're supposed to drop our lifelong quest for individual excellence and combine our money, living space, energy, and time with another person's—and to do it for the rest of our life, till death do us part.

This is the problem we confronted when we first moved in together and Nate couldn't seem to put away his running shoes. It's the problem that grew deeper and more complex with each passing year of our marriage. It's the very same problem so many of the couples we interviewed shared with us. It's the problem that arises when an entire generation is told to be self-reliant, special, and exceptional and then expected to let go of a lifetime of conditioning and somehow seamlessly transition into the project of sharing a life with another human being.

How did our ancestors do it? As we have seen, they had a straightforward and yet utterly unjust solution. In the 80/20 model, they achieved this unity of two separate partners by subverting the individual identity of an entire generation of women. Two became one by empowering the husband to rule over the family like a feudal lord, leaving the wife with no voice, no ambitions, and no easy way out.

Thanks to changing cultural and economic conditions, there's now a broad consensus that the two partners in marriage should be equals. It's an aspiration that isn't always met but has ushered in a new era of marriage, the age of 50/50.

The problem with the 50/50 model is that it has pushed us so far toward the side of individualism and separation that many couples have lost access to the one thing that makes marriage amazing: our ability to connect, share, and experience a taste of oneness. It's a model that tells us to be rational rather than romantic, to be fair rather than generous, and to win individually rather than together.

That begs an essential question. If we're intent on staying separate and safe as individuals, if we want things to be perfectly fair, then why marry or entangle ourselves in a relationship at all? Why not simplify things by building a life alone?

It's a question many people are asking these days. And for many, the answer is that they have indeed reached the end of a marriage or relationship.[1] There's no longer any need to couple up. It's no longer worth indulging the naive idea that they're better off together, as a partnership, than they are apart, as two individuals.

We wrote this book because we believe there's a different answer to this question. True, we could survive and perhaps even thrive as individuals. And yet sharing a life with another opens the door for some of the highest, most meaningful, and sublime experiences available to us as human beings.

We wrote this book because we believe there's a way of engaging in a relationship that allows us to preserve our individual identity while also experiencing the true depth of connection that comes from combining our lives.

The path to an 80/80 marriage or relationship isn't always easy. It requires resisting many of our own hardwired instincts shaped by an individualistic culture. And yet we hope to have shown throughout the course of this book that it's a path all couples can take.

In an age defined by narcissism, self-promotion, and self-protection, the 80/80 model is radical. It's based on the idea that we can achieve the deepest states of connection, intimacy, and happiness by pulling closer instead of going our own way. It's a system designed around the idea that becoming one together is perhaps the greatest source of joy available to us.

As we've seen, the 80/80 model involves two core transformations. The first is a shift in mindset to radical generosity. The second is the structural shift toward shared success in all areas of life. We've experienced the power of these two transformations firsthand; they've changed everything in our marriage and our life. And when we talked with others about their experiences, we discovered we weren't some random marital anomaly.

Most thriving couples point toward these qualities of the 80/80 model as the key to the health of their relationship. They don't talk about their partner with sarcasm or contempt. They brag about them. They talk less about fairness and more about the essential role of small acts of kindness and generosity. They don't talk about their individual accomplishments. They talk about winning together as a team.

None of this is to say that the 80/80 model is the only way to do marriage. Marriage, like life itself, doesn't have a single, one-size-fits-all formula for success.

And yet we live in a unique age with unique challenges. It's a time defined by head-spinning change, extreme stress, and the near-constant pull of digital distractions. It's a time defined by a perpetual state of busyness—that feeling of rushing through each day, having too much to do, and never quite having the time to unwind and simply be together.

It's a time when many couples are searching for a new model of marriage, a way of being together that offers a safe haven from the stress of modern life and access to the experiences that make marriage worth fighting for: ecstatic pleasure, deep connection, and love.

It's time for the 80/80 model.

ACKNOWLEDGMENTS

Something unexpected happened during the writing of this book. In the final month of working on the manuscript, we found ourselves "social distancing" and "sheltering in place" during the initial quarantine of the coronavirus pandemic. Living in near-total isolation turned out to be the perfect pressure test for the ideas in the book, something like the marital equivalent of running an ultramarathon. We slipped out of 80/80 constantly during this time of crisis, but this framework and our efforts to keep coming back to radical generosity and shared success helped us grow together. It offered a sense of direction in the midst of the storm.

This final month of writing also reminded us of the value of community. It reminded us that without the help of so many others, this project would have been quite simply impossible.

The gratitude starts with our parents. Nate's parents, Joe and Margi, hosted countless breakfasts with our daughter, which gave us time to sneak away for morning date hikes. In fact, it was during one of these hikes that the idea for this book was born.

Kaley's parents, Jim and Judy, were on the front line, supporting us both during ordinary life and during the chaos of the final month of writing. Their willingness to help with our temporary homeschool and host sleepovers allowed us to stay connected and focused on bringing this book to the world. Kaley's brother, Paul, and sister, Adela, also helped in countless ways, offering insights about the book and reminding us to never stop laughing at ourselves.

We were also fortunate in the writing of this book to have an amazing team at Penguin Random House. Our editor, Meg Leder, helped us shape this idea from its early stages into its current form. Her wise comments and insights pushed us to think about the 80/80 marriage in new and unexpected ways. Associate editor Amy Sun helped us see the ideas in the manuscript with fresh eyes and uncover many of the blind spots in our thinking. We're also grateful to our literary agent, Nicole Tourtelot, who believed in us and this idea from the very beginning.

This book would not have been possible without the countless conversations we had with married couples who were willing to reveal their inner experience of marriage to the two of us. We interviewed too many couples to name, but we're eternally grateful to all of them for sharing both the joys and the hard truths of their experience of marriage.

We also want to thank our friends and colleagues for their support and feedback throughout the creative process. Eric Langshur, Nate's cofounder at LifeXT and coauthor of *Start Here*, has been a rock-steady source of support, mentorship, and inspiration. Our good friends Priti and Ankit Patel, mentioned in chapter three, were the original early adopters of the 80/80 marriage, testing out each new idea and concept. Cameron Madill blew our mind with his insightful comments on the original draft of the manuscript. Sue Heilbronner helped us see our writing in new ways and was a huge source of support from the very beginning. Jim Kochalka inspired us to stay true to our voice while also staying true to the research on marriage.

We are forever grateful to our inner circle of friends, who are our partners in exploring new ideas and the challenges life brings us: Meredith and Bo Parfet, Liz and Derek Nelson, and Delynn Copley and Pat Hubbell.

Finally, we're grateful to our daughter, the "jo" in Kajona, the one who changed everything.

APPENDIX

Additional Resources

MINDFULNESS

All of the 80/80 marriage practices require the ability to interrupt the often subconscious 80/20 and 50/50 habits we fall into. To develop this ability of noticing your current mindset and shifting it to a more productive state, mindfulness training is essential. For more on beginning a mindfulness practice, see:

- Eric Langshur and Nate Klemp, *Start Here: Master the Lifelong Habit of Wellbeing* (New York: Northstar Way, 2016). This book offers practical guidance on how to use a tool called Notice-Shift-Rewire to turn mindfulness into a regular habit.
- Pema Chödrön, *How to Meditate* (Boulder, CO: Sounds True, 2013). A fantastic guide for beginners interested in learning more about how to meditate.
- Joseph Goldstein, *Mindfulness: A Practical Guide to Awakening* (Boulder, CO: Sounds True, 2013). One of the most comprehensive books on mindfulness practice (perfect for those interested in taking a deep dive into the subject).

CONSCIOUS LIVING AND LEADERSHIP

Your ability to sustain the practice of the 80/80 marriage isn't just about being more mindful. It's also about developing greater consciousness around the way you interact with others. To learn more, see:

- Jim Dethmer, Diana Chapman, and Kaley Warner Klemp, *The 15 Commitments of Conscious Leadership* (Jim Dethmer, Diana Chapman, and Kaley Klemp, 2015). This book outlines fifteen core commitments for becoming a more conscious leader.
- Gay Hendricks, *Conscious Living: Finding Joy in the Real World* (New York: Harper, 2009). This is one of the classics on how to bring this spirit of greater consciousness into all areas of life.

Questioning Your Thoughts

One of the key 80/80 insights is the idea that your mindset determines your experience of marriage. It's an idea that sits at the core of Byron Katie's work. As she likes to put it, "The world is a mirror image of your own mind." To learn more about how you can deepen your 80/80 practice by exploring her Socratic approach of questioning your thoughts, see:

- Byron Katie, *Loving What Is* (New York: Three Rivers Press, 2003).
- Byron Katie, *A Thousand Names for Joy* (New York: Harmony, 2008).

Sex and Eroticism in Marriage

The 80/80 marriage model is based on the idea that the quality of your sex life is closely tied to the quality of your connection in the rest of life. To enhance intimacy, in other words, it's often less about learning new techniques and tools in the bedroom and more about enhancing your mindset and structure in marriage. And yet there are all sorts of powerful techniques related more directly to sex and intimacy that can also supercharge your erotic connection. Here are a few of our favorite approaches:

- David Deida, *The Way of the Superior Man* (Boulder, CO: Sounds True, 2004). This is a classic book on enhancing eroticism through experimenting with the energetic polarities of masculine and feminine.
- Layla Martin, "Epic Lovers," LaylaMartin.com, https://laylamartin .com/epic-lovers-digital-guide. A great free guide with all sorts of practical ways to explore with each other in the bedroom.
- Esther Perel, *Mating in Captivity* (New York: HarperCollins, 2009). A fantastic discussion of the blockages to intimacy we often encounter in modern life as well as the tools we can use to overcome them.

NOTES

Introduction

1. A quick note on methodology for those who are interested. We conducted more than one hundred interviews with people who were either (1) married, (2) divorced, (3) in a committed intimate relationship, or (4) experts in the marriage space. With couples, we asked participants to spend thirty minutes with us and requested that each partner speak to us separately. In some cases, couples preferred to do the interview together, during a single thirty-minute conversation. We conducted these thirty-minute interviews by phone and used the following format: During the first five minutes, we introduced the project. For the remainder of the time, we asked a semi-structured list of interview questions. We started by interviewing people we knew, but we would then ask our interviewees if they would be willing to introduce us to other couples, which expanded our reach far beyond our network of social and professional contacts. To ensure a diverse sample, we actively reached out to same-sex couples, gender-nonconforming couples, interracial couples, couples in which one or both partners were ethnic minorities, couples from a mix of socioeconomic classes, and couples with a mix of religious and political views.
2. We are not the first to see marriage as progressing along three stages. In fact, we are grateful to the pathbreaking work of relationships expert David Deida, the first person we have found to outline a three-stage progression. We share his view of a three-stage process. And yet his relationship theory leads to a radically different destination. Deida thinks the third stage is about gender polarity—men and women returning to the essential energies of the masculine and feminine. By contrast, we see this third, more aspirational stage (the 80/80 model) as culminating in a new relationship mindset (radical generosity), a new structure (shared success), and a new set of habits and rituals to sustain this shift. For his seminal book on this subject, see David Deida, *The Way of the Superior Man* (Boulder, CO: Sounds True, 2017).
3. *Primary-secondary* is a term coined by marriage researcher Jennifer Petriglieri. She argues that most couples fall into one of three categories: *primary-secondary*, in which one person's career takes priority; *double-primary*, in which couples juggle two primary careers; and *turn taking*, in which partners alternate between primary and secondary positions. See Jennifer Petriglieri, *Couples That Work* (Cambridge, MA: Harvard Business School Press, 2019), 70–73.

Chapter 1

1. Edward Podolsky, *Sex Today in Wedded Life* (New York: Simon Publications, 1945), 237.
2. Podolsky, *Sex Today in Wedded Life*, 237.

3. Jim Daly and Paul Batura, "Ten Commandments for Husbands and Wives," May 3, 2017, *Focus on the Family* (blog), https://jimdaly.focusonthefamily.com/ten-commandments -husbands-wives/?utm_source=facebook&utm_medium=social&utm_campaign=fs _dalyblog_may_3&refcd=138602&fbclid=IwAR2ODdy0QMD4IalEMFvznJHcw t9UhRYHMXliS-kpE8Ll14PJ5R9xWWTlVzo.

4. Stephanie Coontz, *Marriage, a History* (New York: Penguin, 2005), 110–11; Jan Luiten van Zanden, Tine De Moor, and Sarah Carmichael, *Capital Women: The European Marriage Pattern, Female Empowerment and Economic Development in Western Europe, 1300–1800* (New York: Oxford University Press, 2019).

5. Sheryl Sandberg, *Lean In: Women, Work, and the Will to Lead* (New York: Knopf, 2013).

6. See, for instance, "Women Had Higher Median Earnings Than Men in Relatively Few Occupations in 2018," US Bureau of Labor Statistics, March 22, 2019, https://www.bls .gov/opub/ted/2019/women-had-higher-median-earnings-than-men-in-relatively-few -occupations-in-2018.htm; Benjamin Artz, Amanda Goodall, and Andrew J. Oswald, "Research: Women Ask for Raises as Often as Men, but Are Less Likely to Get Them," *Harvard Business Review*, June 25, 2018, https://hbr.org/2018/06/research-women-ask -for-raises-as-often-as-men-but-are-less-likely-to-get-them.

7. "Gender Equality Universally Embraced, but Inequalities Acknowledged," Pew Research Center, July 1, 2010, https://www.pewresearch.org/global/2010/07/01/gender -equality.

8. Gretchen Livingston and Kim Parker, "8 Facts About American Dads," Pew Research Center, June 12, 2019, https://www.pewresearch.org/fact-tank/2019/06/12/fathers-day-facts/.

9. Judith Shulevitz, "Mom: The Designated Worrier," *New York Times*, May 8, 2015, https://www.nytimes.com/2015/05/10/opinion/sunday/judith-shulevitz-mom-the -designated-worrier.html.

10. We interviewed Dr. Hochschild, and it's worth noting that she actually limits the category of emotional labor to work in the public sphere—i.e., the emotional burden of laborers such as flight attendants, secretaries, and service employees who interact face-to-face or "voice-to-voice" with the public. She uses the term *emotional work*, by contrast, to describe the form of labor in the household. In contemporary discussions of the idea, however, *emotional labor* is the term most commonly used for household labor, so we are following this convention. See Arlie Russell Hochschild, *The Managed Heart* (Berkeley: University of California Press, 2012), 7. For a more contemporary discussion of emotional labor, see Gemma Hartley, "Women Aren't Nags—We're Just Fed Up," *Harper's Bazaar*, September 27, 2017, https://www.harpersbazaar.com/culture/features/a1206 3822/emotional-labor-gender-equality; Gemma Hartley, *Fed Up: Emotional Labor, Women, and the Way Forward* (New York: HarperOne, 2018).

Chapter 2

1. Alix Kates Shulman, "A Marriage Agreement," *A Marriage Agreement and Other Essays* (New York: Open Road, 2012), 9.

2. Shulman, "A Marriage Agreement," 9–14.

3. Shulman, "A Marriage Agreement," 15–37.

4. Coontz, *Marriage, a History*, 230.

5. Mitra Toossi and Teresa L. Morisi, "Women in the Workforce Before, During, and After the Great Recession," US Bureau of Labor Statistics, July 2017, https://www.bls.gov /spotlight/2017/women-in-the-workforce-before-during-and-after-the-great-recession /pdf/women-in-the-workforce-before-during-and-after-the-great-recession.pdf.

6. A. W. Geiger and Kim Parker, "For Women's History Month, a Look at Gender Gains— and Gaps—in the U.S.," Pew Research Center, March 15, 2018, https://www.pew research.org/fact-tank/2018/03/15/for-womens-history-month-a-look-at-gender-gains

-and-gaps-in-the-u-s. For a helpful discussion of how these changes in marriage impacted same-sex marriages, as well as a powerful moral argument for same-sex marriage, see Stephen Macedo, *Just Married* (Princeton, NJ: Princeton University Press, 2017).

7. For an excellent overview of this literature, see Scott Coltrane, "Research on Household Labor: Modeling and Measuring the Social Embeddedness of Routine Family Work," *Journal of Marriage and Family* 62, no. 4 (2000): 1208–33.

8. Julie E. Press and Eleanor Townsley, "Wives' and Husbands' Housework Reporting: Gender, Class, and Social Desirability," *Gender and Society* 12, no. 2 (1998): 188–218. For a more contemporary study with similar findings, see Jill E. Yavorsky, Claire M. Kamp Dush, and Sarah J. Schoppe-Sullivan, "The Production of Inequality: The Gender Division of Labor Across the Transition to Parenthood," *Journal of Marriage and Family* 77, no. 3 (2015): 662–79.

Chapter 5

1. For Chapman's original articulation of the five love languages, see Gary Chapman, *The Five Love Languages* (Chicago: Northfield, 1992).

Chapter 6

1. "Love Lab," Gottman Institute, https://www.gottman.com/love-lab.

2. Emily Esfahani Smith, "Masters of Love," *The Atlantic*, June 12, 2014, https://www.the atlantic.com/health/archive/2014/06/happily-ever-after/372573.

3. Smith, "Masters of Love."

4. Kyle Benson, "The Magic Relationship Ratio, According to Science," Gottman Institute, https://www.gottman.com/blog/the-magic-relationship-ratio-according-science.

5. "Marriage and Couples," Gottman Institute, https://www.gottman.com/about/research /couples.

6. A. Vaish, T. Grossmann, and A. Woodward, "Not All Emotions Are Created Equal: The Negativity Bias in Social-Emotional Development," *Psychological Bulletin* 134, no. 3 (2008): 383–403. For a more popular account of this phenomenon, see Rick Hanson, *Buddha's Brain* (New York: New Harbinger, 2009).

7. Robert Sapolsky, *Why Zebras Don't Get Ulcers* (New York: Holt, 2004).

Chapter 7

1. Mark Savage and Jill Savage, *No More Perfect Marriages: 10-Day Blog Series*, https:// attachments.convertkitcdn.com/21710/0ecb81d8-b1ba-47ad-8b4e-919bfa1600df /No%20More%20Perfect%20Marriages%20Blog%20Series%20PDF%20.pdf.

2. Mark Savage and Jill Savage, *No More Perfect Marriages* (New York: Moody, 2017).

3. Gay Hendricks and Kathlyn Hendricks, *Conscious Loving* (New York: Bantam, 1992), 115.

4. For Carlson's research on the link between communication and sharing household tasks, see Daniel Carlson, "Division of Domestic Labor, Communication, and Couples' Relationship Satisfaction" (working paper, University of Utah, Salt Lake City, 2020). For his research on the correlation between equality and sexual satisfaction, see Daniel L. Carlson, Sarah Hanson, and Andrea Fitzroy, "The Division of Child Care, Sexual Intimacy, and Relationship Quality in Couples," *Gender and Society* 30, no. 3 (2016): 442–66.

5. Christine Webb, Maya Rossignac-Milon, and E. Tory Higgins, "Stepping Forward Together: Could Walking Facilitate Interpersonal Conflict Resolution?" *American Psychologist* 72, no. 4 (2017): 374–85.

Chapter 10

1. Gloria Steinem, "Commencement Speech to the Class of 1998," Wellesley College, 1988, https://www.wellesley.edu/events/commencement/archives/1988Commencement/commencementaddress.
2. Ty Rogers (@_TyRogers_), Twitter, April 1, 2020, https://twitter.com/_tyrogers_/status/1245503349010477056?lang=en.
3. Stewart Friedman, Elizabeth Grace Saunders, Peter Bregman, and Daisy Wademan Dowling, *HBR Guide to Work-Life Balance* (Cambridge, MA: Havard Business Review Press, 2019).
4. Greg McKeown, *Essentialism: The Disciplined Pursuit of Less* (New York: Currency, 2014).

Chapter 11

1. Stan Tatkin, *Wired for Love* (New York: New Harbinger, 2012), 119–38.
2. For an excellent discussion of the boundaries problem as well as a much more extensive list of the various tactics for saying no, see McKeown, *Essentialism*, 140–43.

Chapter 12

1. Mark Hodkinson, *Queen: The Early Years* (New York: Omnibus Press, 2009).
2. Hodkinson, *Queen*.
3. "Queen: The Music. The Life. The Rhapsody," *Life Magazine Book* 18, no. 22 (2018).
4. This idea of "arbitrary" power diminishing freedom runs throughout the republican tradition of political theory. For an excellent relatively recent account of freedom as "non-domination," see Philip Pettit, *Republicanism: A Theory of Freedom and Government* (New York: Oxford University Press, 1998).
5. Laina Bay-Cheng, "Who Wears the Pants in a Relationship Matters—Especially If You're a Woman," The Conversation, April 9, 2017, http://theconversation.com/who-wears-the-pants-in-a-relationship-matters-especially-if-youre-a-woman-74401. For her peer-reviewed article, see Laina Bay-Cheng, Eugene Maguin, and Anne E. Bruns, "Who Wears the Pants: The Implications of Gender and Power for Youth Heterosexual Relationships," *Journal of Sex Research 55*, no. 1 (2018): 7–20.
6. Léa Rose Emery, "How Should You Really Be Splitting the Bills with Your Partner?" *Brides*, January 12, 2020, https://www.brides.com/story/how-should-you-really-be-splitting-the-bills-with-your-partner.

Chapter 13

1. Esther Perel, *Mating in Captivity* (New York: HarperCollins, 2009), 75.
2. Belinda Luscombe, "Why Are We All Having So Little Sex?" *Time*, October 26, 2018, https://time.com/5297145/is-sex-dead.
3. Jean M. Twenge, Ryne A. Sherman, and Brooke E. Wells, "Declines in Sexual Frequency Amount American Adults, 1989–2014," *Archives of Sexual Behavior* 46, no. 8 (2017): 2389–401, https://link.springer.com/article/10.1007/s10508-017-0953-1. For an account of the current "sex recession," see Kate Julian, "Why Are Young People Having So Little Sex?" *The Atlantic*, December 2018, https://www.theatlantic.com/magazine/archive/2018/12/the-sex-recession/573949.
4. L. C. Day et al., "To Do It or Not to Do It? How Communally Motivated People Navigate Sexual Interdependence Dilemmas," *Personality and Social Psychology Bulletin* 4, no. 6 (2015): 791–804. U. S. Rehman et al., "Marital Satisfaction and Communication

Behaviors During Sexual and Nonsexual Conflict Discussions in Newlywed Couples: A Pilot Study," *Journal of Sex and Marital Therapy* 37, no. 2 (2011): 94–103.

5. See, for instance, Samuel L. Perry and Cyrus Schleifer, "Till Porn Do Us Part? A Longitudinal Examination of Pornography Use and Divorce," *Journal of Sex Research* 55, no. 3 (2018): 284–96.

6. Perel, *Mating in Captivity*, 142.

7. Heidi Stevens, "Want a Better Sex Life? Choreplay Definitely Works," *Chicago Tribune*, August 26, 2015, https://www.chicagotribune.com/lifestyles/ct-egalitarian-marriage-better -sex-balancing-20150826-column.html.

8. Tony DiLorenzo and Alisa DiLorenzo, *7 Days of Sex Challenge: How to Rock Your Sex Life and Your Marriage* (Amazon CreateSpace, 2013).

Chapter 14

1. Gene Landrum, *Profiles of Female Genius* (New York: Prometheus Books, 1994), 323.

2. Gloria Steinem, *The Truth Will Set You Free, but First It Will Piss You Off!* (New York: Random House, 2019), 31.

3. Jessica Valenti, "Kids Don't Damage Women's Careers—Men Do," Medium, September 13, 2018, https://gen.medium.com/kids-dont-damage-women-s-careers-men-do-eb07 cba689b8.

4. Gay and Kathlyn Hendricks, "The Art of Commitment," *Psychotherapy Networker*, September/October 2001, https://www.psychotherapynetworker.org/magazine/article/869 /the-art-of-commitment. To learn more about how this concept applies to marriage and life, see Gay and Kathlyn Hendricks, *Conscious Loving* (New York: Bantam, 1992); Gay Hendricks, *Conscious Living* (New York: Harper, 2009); Gay Hendricks, *The Big Leap* (New York: HarperOne, 2010).

Chapter 15

1. William James, "Habit," in *The Writings of William James*, ed. John J. McDermott (Chicago: University of Chicago Press, 1977), 12.

2. Charles Duhigg, *The Power of Habit* (New York: Random House, 2014).

3. Duhigg, *The Power of Habit*.

4. Nate's book with Eric Langshur, *Start Here*, offers a detailed exploration into how to build the key habits of well-being and resilience; see Eric Langshur and Nate Klemp, *Start Here: Master the Lifelong Habit of Wellbeing* (New York: Northstar Way, 2016). One of the classic books in the field is B. J. Fogg, *Tiny Habits: The Small Changes That Change Everything* (New York: Houghton Mifflin Harcourt, 2019). See also James Clear, *Atomic Habits* (New York: Avery, 2018).

5. Brad Feld and Amy Batchelor, *Startup Life* (New York: Wiley, 2013), 79.

6. Linda Stone, "Continuous Partial Attention," LindaStone.net, https://lindastone.net/qa /continuous-partial-attention.

Epilogue

1. See, for example, Mandy Len Catron, "What You Lose When You Gain a Spouse," *The Atlantic*, July 2, 2019, https://www.theatlantic.com/family/archive/2019/07/case-against -marriage/591973/.